GET READY TO READ

A Skills-Based Reader

Karen Blanchard

Christine Root

Longman

This book is dedicated to our students—past, present, and future.

Get Ready to Read: A Skills-Based Reader

Pearson Education, 10 Bank Street, White Plains, NY 10606

Executive editor: Laura Le Dréan
Acquisitions editor: Lucille M. Kennedy
Development editors: Margot Gramer, Andrea Bryant
Project editor: Helen B. Ambrosio
Production coordinator: Melissa Leyva
Director of manufacturing: Patrice Fraccio
Senior manufacturing buyer: Dave Dickey
Cover design: Pat Wosczyk
Text composition: Laserwords
Photo research: Dana Klinek
Photo and text credits appear on page ix.
Cover photo: © April/Getty Images
Illustrations: Peter Grau, Jill C. Wood

Library of Congress Cataloging-in-Publication Data

Blanchard, Karen Lourie,
    Get ready to read : a skills–based reader / by Karen Blanchard and Christine Root.
      p. cm.
    Includes index
    ISBN 0–13–177648–7
    1. English language—Textbooks for foreign speakers. 2. Reading—Problems, exercises, etc. 3. Readers.
I. Root, Christine Baker, 1945– II. Title.

PE1128, B58647 2005
428.6'4—dc22

2004024271

ISBN: 0–13–177648–7

LONGMAN ON THE **WEB**

Longman.com offers online resources for teachers and students. Access our Companion Websites, our online catalog, and our local offices around the world.

Visit us at **longman.com**.

Printed in the United States of America
  8 9 10— *V001* —10

Contents

Scope and Sequence

CHAPTER	READING SKILLS	VOCABULARY SKILLS	MAIN READING	HAVE SOME FUN
1 What's It All About?	Finding the topic	Using a dictionary — alphabetizing; guide words	*Interview with Mong Meng*	Doing an information gap activity
2 Look It Over	Previewing, predicting, and making connections	Using a dictionary— Definitions	*What Color Are You Wearing?*	Completing a crossword puzzle
3 Read for Meaning	Main ideas, supporting details	Dictionary skills—parts of speech	*Picture This: Photography Past and Present*	Doing a word search
4 Find the Order	Recognizing time order	Using context clues	*Things Happen for a Reason*	Making up a group story
5 Read Quickly	Scanning	Using word maps	*Let's Dance*	Playing a picture memory game
6 Evaluate Information	Distinguishing facts from opinions	Suffixes	*Beckham: A Soccer Superstar*	Doing an information gap activity
7 Use the Clues	Making inferences	Prefixes	*My Travels by Train in the Western United States*	Completing a maze

v

Introduction

Like its companion writing series, *Ready to Write*, the **Ready to Read** series comprises three task-based, skill-building textbooks for students of English. Also like its sister series, the reading series is skills-based and user-friendly, a series that both teachers and students will find easy to follow and use. **Get Ready to Read**, the beginning level book in the series, focuses on helping students understand and practice the basic reading skills required for efficient, independent, academic as well as pleasure reading.

THE APPROACH

The books in the **Ready to Read** series are made up of task-based chapters, each of which has reading and vocabulary skill-building as its primary focus. In this series we started by choosing the reading and vocabulary skills we wanted to teach in each chapter and then selected readings for their value in helping students understand and practice those specific skills.

As a skill is presented, paintings, photographs, graphics, examples, and short texts, both prose and nonprose, are used to illustrate that skill and provide practice. Each chapter opens with a pictorial representation of a reading skill to give students a non-verbal reference point. The reading skill is then practiced throughout the text, recycled and reinforced in every subsequent chapter.

Like the *Ready to Write* series, the exercises in the **Ready to Read** series involve the students actively. Proficient reading, like writing, requires a network of complex skills that can be taught, practiced, and improved. This series teaches competency in these skills by taking students on a step-by-step progression through the reading skills and word attack strategies that promote efficient and effective reading, and then by continuously recycling the practice of those skills. Students read with a purpose, be it to increase reading efficiency, summarize an article, apply the skill presented in the chapter at hand or review those skills presented in previous chapters.

In addition to demonstrating comprehension through standard exercises, students are asked to make a graphic organizer or visual representation of each article by completing a chart, graph, table, or outline as they read. These graphic organizers help students focus on the underlying structure of the reading and understand the interrelationships among ideas.

We hope you find the exercises in this book useful as you help your students **Get Ready to Read**!

Acknowledgments

For their help in envisioning, supporting, and creating this series, we thank Laura Le Dréan, Lucille M. Kennedy, Margot Gramer, Andrea Bryant, Dana Klinek, and Helen Ambrosio at Longman, as well as our friends, family, and colleagues: Daniel Blanchard; Diane Englund; Andrew Gulliford; Candace Kerner; Sharon McKay; Lynn Meng; and David, Matt, and Ian Root.

Thanks also to the reviewers whose comments on early drafts of this book were very helpful: Marsha Abramovich, Tidewater Community College, Virginia Beach, VA; Kay Ferrell, Santa Ana College, Santa Ana, CA; Mary Jane Onnen, Glendale Community College, Glendale, AZ.

The visual arts play a pivotal role in this book. For their generosity of time and spirit we thank Larry Berman at the Museum of Fine Arts, Boston, and William Wegman.

About the Authors

Karen Blanchard and **Christine Root** each have taught English language instruction at the university level for over twenty years. Karen has an M.S.Ed in TESOL from the University of Pennsylvania, and Christine has an M.Ed in English Education from the University of Massachusetts, Boston. They began their textbook collaboration with the *Ready to Write* series while they were lecturers at the University of Pennsylvania. They have since written many reading and writing skills books and continue to enjoy working together to create English language textbooks for students around the world.

Credits

CHAPTER 1

What's It All About?
Finding the Topic

Look at the picture. Discuss what you see with a partner. Then answer the question.

What is the picture about?

    a. a beautiful day
    b. a bicycle race
    c. learning to ride a bicycle

When you decided that the picture was about "b. a bicycle race," you found the topic. You should also look for the topic when you read. Knowing the topic of a reading will help you understand it better. It will also help you remember what you read.

Sharpen Your Reading Skills

FINDING THE TOPIC

A topic is a word or phrase that tells what something is about. To find the topic of a reading ask yourself, "What or who is the reading about?" The answer will be the topic. You should always look for the topic when you read.

 The subject of a movie or a conversation is called the **topic**. The subject of something such as a magazine article, an e-mail, or even a list of words is also called a topic. A topic answers the question, "What or who is it about?" The topic is usually just a word or a short phrase.

Finding the Topic of a List

A. One word in each list answers the question, "What is this list about?" That word is the topic of the list. Circle the topic of each list.

Example

Japanese
Spanish
(languages)
Arabic
English

1. Korea	2. dog	3. spring	4. sports
Mexico	lion	seasons	tennis
India	elephant	fall	soccer
China	animals	winter	basketball
countries	mouse	summer	golf

B. Read each list and choose the best topic from the box below. Write it on the line. Ask yourself, "What is this list about?" The answer is the topic.

times   names   days
months   furniture   rooms

Example

Topic: _____names_____

Keiko

Molly

José

Abdulla

Daniel

1. **Topic:** _____

desk

chair

table

sofa

bookcase

2. **Topic:** _____

3:30

noon

four o'clock

midnight

7:00 A.M.

3. **Topic:** _____

kitchen

dining room

den

living room

library

4. **Topic:** _____

Wednesday

Monday

Thursday

Sunday

Friday

5. **Topic:** _____

May

June

July

January

March

C. Read each list and choose the best topic from the box below. Write it on the line.

> things to eat with   kinds of cars   types of music
> parts of a car   musical instruments ways to communicate

1. Topic: _____
   flute
   piano
   violin
   guitar
   drum

2. Topic: _____
   wheels
   trunk
   brake
   horn
   engine

3. Topic: _____
   knife
   chopsticks
   fork
   spoon

4. Topic: _____
   Honda
   Volkswagen
   Ford
   Mercedes Benz
   Kia

5. Topic: _____
   telephone
   fax
   e-mail
   letter
   text message

6. Topic: _____
   jazz
   rock 'n' roll
   classical
   hip-hop
   blues

D. Think about each of the following topics and then write your own list. Share your list with a partner.

1. Topic: My Hobbies

   _____
   _____
   _____
   _____

2. Topic: My Favorite Movies

   _____
   _____
   _____
   _____

3. Topic: My Favorite Foods

   _____
   _____
   _____
   _____

4. Topic: Places I Want to Visit

   _____
   _____
   _____
   _____

Finding the Topic of a Poster

E. Look at the five Internet links below. The links are the names of topics. Which poster would you find for each link? Write the correct number on the line.

—— <u>sports poster</u>

—— <u>animal poster</u>

—— <u>movie poster</u>

—— <u>music poster</u>

—— <u>travel poster</u>

1.

2.

3.

4.

5.

Finding the Topic of a Conversation

F. Read the following short conversations. Write the topic of each conversation on the line. Ask yourself, "What are the people talking about?"

Example

Alex: What did you do last night?

Bill: I went to my cousin's twenty-first birthday party.

Alex: Did you have a good time?

Bill: Yeah. It was great. The food was delicious and the music was fantastic. Everyone danced and ate the whole night. All the guests stayed at the party until 3:00 in the morning.

Topic: <u>A birthday party</u>

---

1. **Linda:** Did you go to the soccer game yesterday?

   Pam: Yeah. It was really exciting. Why didn't you go?

   Linda: I wanted to go, but I had to work. What was the final score?

   Pam: It was a close game. Our team made a goal in the last minute, and we won 3 to 2.

   Topic: _____

2. **Becky:** My boyfriend surprised me yesterday.

   Jane: What did he do?

   Becky: He gave me a kitten. She is so sweet. She's only five weeks old.

   Jane: That's a great surprise. What does she look like?

   Becky: She has orange and white fur with big green eyes.

   Jane: What is her name?

   Becky: I named her Pumpkin.

   Topic: _____

3. **Ben:** How is your new job at the library?

   Sam: I've only been there two weeks, but I really like it.

   Ben: That's great. What do you do?

   Sam: I work at the check out desk. Sometimes, I help people find books. When it isn't busy, I can study or read.

   Ben: It sounds like a perfect job for a student.

   Topic: _____

Finding the Topic of an E-mail

G. The topic of an e-mail is written on the subject line. Write the topic of each of the following e-mails.

Example

> **From:** Jane
>
> **Date:** Wednesday, September 24, 2004, 9:00 A.M.
>
> **To:** Christine
>
> **Subject:** _Concert ticket_
>
> Hi Christine,
>
> I have an extra ticket to "The Sounds of Brazil" concert tonight. Can you come with me? Call me and let me know if you can use the ticket.
>
> Jane

1.

> **From:** Dan
>
> **Date:** Wednesday, September 24, 2004, 9:00 A.M.
>
> **To:** Ian
>
> **Subject:** _____
>
> Hi Ian,
>
> I just bought a new car! It's a red convertible. Will you be home tonight? I'll come over and give you a ride in my new car.
>
> Dan

2.

From: Susan

Date: Wednesday, September 24, 2004, 9:00 A.M.

To: Gary

Subject: _____

Dear Gary,

Here's the homework we have for tomorrow. Read Chapter 7 in the history book. Do the problems on page 65 in geometry. Also learn the new vocabulary words for a quiz in Spanish. Call me if you have any questions.

Susan

3.

From: Mary

Date: Wednesday, September 24, 2004, 9:00 A.M.

To: Randy

Subject: _____

Randy,

I'm all settled in my new apartment. Here is my new phone number and address:

Mary Star
160 Second Avenue
Apartment 2A
Silver Springs, MD 34012
Phone: 316-555-0982

Call me soon.

Mary

Finding the Topic of a City Guide

H. Look at the city guide for Savannah, Georgia. Choose the best topic of each section and write it on the line. Follow the example.

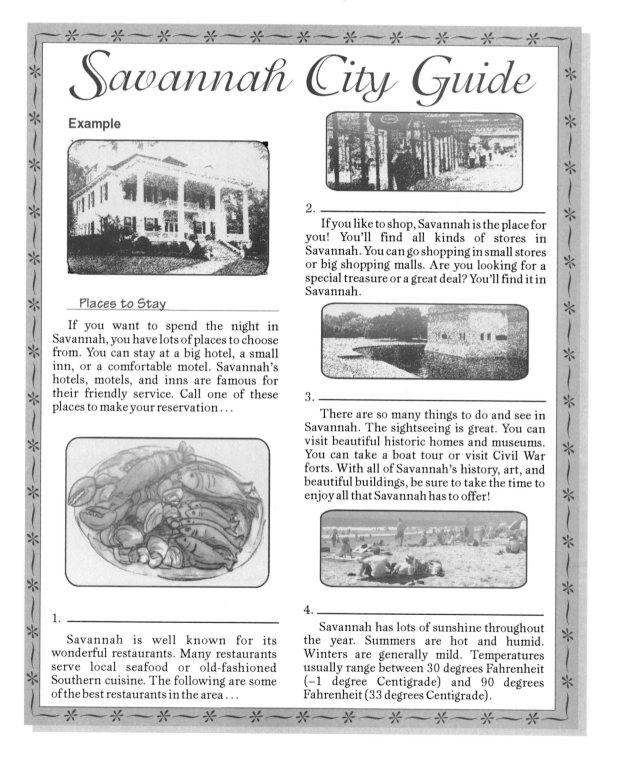

Savannah City Guide

Example

Places to Stay

If you want to spend the night in Savannah, you have lots of places to choose from. You can stay at a big hotel, a small inn, or a comfortable motel. Savannah's hotels, motels, and inns are famous for their friendly service. Call one of these places to make your reservation...

1. _____

Savannah is well known for its wonderful restaurants. Many restaurants serve local seafood or old-fashioned Southern cuisine. The following are some of the best restaurants in the area...

2. _____

If you like to shop, Savannah is the place for you! You'll find all kinds of stores in Savannah. You can go shopping in small stores or big shopping malls. Are you looking for a special treasure or a great deal? You'll find it in Savannah.

3. _____

There are so many things to do and see in Savannah. The sightseeing is great. You can visit beautiful historic homes and museums. You can take a boat tour or visit Civil War forts. With all of Savannah's history, art, and beautiful buildings, be sure to take the time to enjoy all that Savannah has to offer!

4. _____

Savannah has lots of sunshine throughout the year. Summers are hot and humid. Winters are generally mild. Temperatures usually range between 30 degrees Fahrenheit (–1 degree Centigrade) and 90 degrees Fahrenheit (33 degrees Centigrade).

Finding the Topic of a Paragraph

Most English writing is organized into paragraphs. A **paragraph** is a group of sentences about one topic. In longer readings, writers start a new paragraph every time they start a new topic. One way for you to find the topic of a paragraph is to look for a word or phrase that is repeated often. That word or phrase is the topic. Another way is to pretend you want to tell a friend about something you just read using only one word or phrase. That word or phrase is the topic.

I. Choose the topic of each paragraph from the list below. Remember to ask yourself, "Who or what is the paragraph about?"

Example

Florida is a wonderful place to visit. The weather is warm for most of the year. There are also many beautiful beaches where you can swim and enjoy sitting in the sun. Another popular place is Disney World, which millions of people visit every year. With all these attractions, Florida is a perfect place to spend a vacation.

a. vacations
ⓑ Florida
c. Disney World

1. There are many popular sports in the United States. Baseball has always been a favorite sport, and most children learn to play baseball in school. Many people also love to play basketball, and there are basketball courts in almost every neighborhood. The most popular American game is football. Football games are a big event at most schools and colleges, and many people watch football every week on television. Americans spend a lot of time playing and watching sports.

a. sports in the United States
b. sports on television
c. football

2. Doctors suggest several ways to lose weight. One way to lose weight is to eat more fruits and vegetables and less fat. Another way is to drink a lot of water, at least eight glasses a day. Finally, it's important to get enough exercise such as walking or running. If we follow this advice, we'll feel better and have more energy.

   a. eating fruits and vegetables
   b. how to exercise
   c. ways to lose weight

3. Finding a job isn't always easy, but there are several steps that can be helpful. A good way to start is to look at ads in the newspaper. There are also jobs listed on the Internet. A college counselor can also give you information about jobs. Finally, it's a good idea to talk to all of your friends and relatives. They might know of a job opening. Finding a job can take time, so don't feel bad—just keep looking!

   a. finding a job
   b. the best jobs
   c. working in the United States

4. One of the biggest names in American entertainment is Walt Disney. Disney was famous for his cartoon characters, especially Mickey Mouse. Disney created popular children's films such as *Cinderella, Snow White*, and *101 Dalmatians*. He won thirty-nine Academy Awards over the course of his career. Disney also dreamed of opening a big, clean amusement park. In 1955, he opened Disneyland, in California. Disney is remembered for creating the first sound cartoon, the first all-color cartoon, and the first animated movie. In his later years, Walt Disney spoke about the success of his company and reminded everyone, "It all started with a mouse."

   a. children's movies
   b. American entertainment
   c. Walt Disney

Be an Active Reader

BEFORE YOU READ

A. What are your hobbies? Put a check next to your hobbies. Then discuss your hobbies with a partner.

- ☐ photography
- ☐ reading
- ☐ playing computer games
- ☐ collecting coins, stamps, dolls, or other objects
- ☐ painting
- ☐ fishing
- ☐ sewing, knitting, crafts
- ☐ gardening
- ☐ exercising
- ☐ golf
- ☐ other

B. Talk to a partner. Discuss the things you like to do in your free time. What things do you like to do outdoors? What things do you like to do indoors?

C. Find out what the three most popular hobbies in your class are.

Preview the Vocabulary

The words in the box are boldfaced in the interview. Work with a partner and do the exercise that follows.

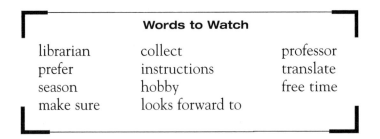

Words to Watch		
librarian	collect	professor
prefer	instructions	translate
season	hobby	free time
make sure	looks forward to	

D. Read the following sentences. Then match the boldfaced words and phrases with the definitions below. Write the correct letter in the space provided. If you need more help, read the sentence in the interview where the word appears and think about how it is used.

_____ 1. The **librarian** helped me find the book I needed.

_____ 2. We **collect** postage stamps from all around the world.

_____ 3. Our English **professor** is my favorite teacher.

_____ 4. My sister likes adventure stories, but I **prefer** comedies.

_____ 5. Please read the **instructions** before you play the game.

_____ 6. Can you **translate** this letter into Korean for me?

_____ 7. Summer is my favorite **season**.

_____ 8. I take pictures as a **hobby**.

_____ 9. We like to relax and watch TV in our **free time**.

_____10. Please **make sure** the door is locked when you leave the apartment.

_____11. He **looks forward** to going skiing every winter.

    a. to like something more than something else

    b. a teacher at a university or college

    c. someone who works in a library

    d. to change speech or writing from one language to another

    e. to get and keep things of a particular kind that interest you

    f. an activity that you enjoy doing when you are not working

    g. one of the four main periods in the year: winter, spring, summer, or fall

    h. to be excited and happy about something that is going to happen

    i. to check that something is true or that something has been done

    j. time when you are not busy doing other things

    k. information that tells how to do or make something

Read with a Purpose

You are going to read an interview with Mong Meng. Mong is from China. He moved to the United States in 1984. He studied literature and library science in the United States. He is now the director of a library at an American university. He keeps busy with his job and all his hobbies.

Write three questions you'd like to ask about Mong.

> **Example**
>
> What was hard for him when he came here?

1. _____

2. _____

3. _____

As you read, complete the chart on the next page by putting a check next to the topics Mong talks about in the interview.

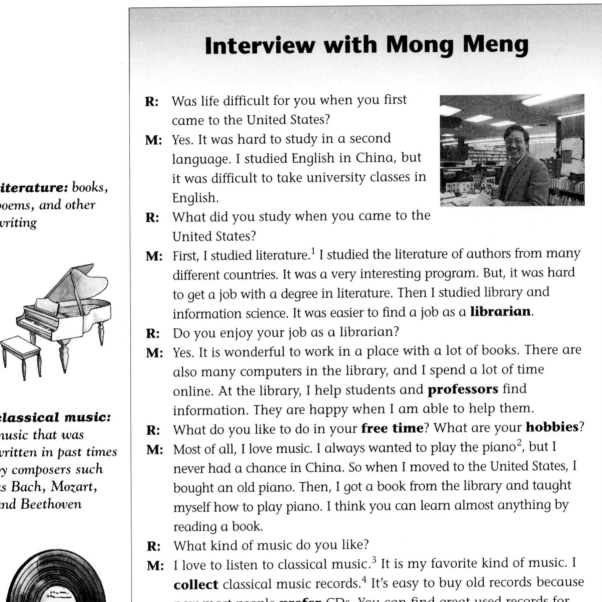

Interview with Mong Meng

R: Was life difficult for you when you first came to the United States?

M: Yes. It was hard to study in a second language. I studied English in China, but it was difficult to take university classes in English.

R: What did you study when you came to the United States?

M: First, I studied literature.[1] I studied the literature of authors from many different countries. It was a very interesting program. But, it was hard to get a job with a degree in literature. Then I studied library and information science. It was easier to find a job as a **librarian**.

R: Do you enjoy your job as a librarian?

M: Yes. It is wonderful to work in a place with a lot of books. There are also many computers in the library, and I spend a lot of time online. At the library, I help students and **professors** find information. They are happy when I am able to help them.

R: What do you like to do in your **free time**? What are your **hobbies**?

M: Most of all, I love music. I always wanted to play the piano[2], but I never had a chance in China. So when I moved to the United States, I bought an old piano. Then, I got a book from the library and taught myself how to play piano. I think you can learn almost anything by reading a book.

R: What kind of music do you like?

M: I love to listen to classical music.[3] It is my favorite kind of music. I **collect** classical music records.[4] It's easy to buy old records because now most people **prefer** CDs. You can find great used records for just a few dollars. I've been collecting records for over ten years. Now I have about 2,000 records.

[1] **literature:** books, poems, and other writing

[2]

[3] **classical music:** music that was written in past times by composers such as Bach, Mozart, and Beethoven

[4]

R: What kind of stereo[5] do you have?

M: I built my own stereo. I followed **instructions** and pictures in books. I saved a lot of money, and I made my stereo exactly the way I wanted it. Every night I listen to several hours of classical music on the stereo I built myself.

R: Do you have any other hobbies?

M: Yes. I enjoy doing Chinese calligraphy.[6] In China, many people practice calligraphy, the art of writing with ink brushes. I feel calm and peaceful when I am doing calligraphy. I also like to write poetry.

R: Do you write your poems in English?

M: No. Usually I write my poems in Chinese. Sometimes I **translate** them into English. I also translate English poetry into Chinese for Chinese books and magazines.

R: Those sound like indoor hobbies. Do you ever go outside?

M: Of course. I love gardening. I have planted hundreds of flowers in my garden. I **make sure** some flowers are blooming in almost every **season**. That way, there is always a lot of color in the garden.

R: Anything else?

M: Another hobby I enjoy is photography. I love to take photographs of nature in different seasons of the year. I take them in the winter, spring, summer, and fall. I have lots of photos of the trees in our yard.

R: Do you know how to print your own photos?

M: Yes, but only black and white photographs, not color.

R: Did you learn how to do this by reading a book?

M: Of course!

R: Looking back at your life, do you have any regrets?

M: Not really. I think it's better not to worry too much about the past. It's better to enjoy the present and **look forward to** the future.

5

[6]**calligraphy:** *the art of writing using special pens or brushes*

	Yes	No
his family and friends		
his job		
the music he likes		
photography		
books		
sports he plays		
poetry		
his pets		
gardening		
food		

AFTER YOU READ

Check Your Comprehension

A. True or False? Write T (True) or F (False) next to each statement.

Example

____T____ Mong studied literature and library and information science.

_____ **1.** Mong likes his job as a librarian.
_____ **2.** Mong bought an expensive stereo.
_____ **3.** Mong writes most of his poems in English.
_____ **4.** Mong enjoys poetry and photography.
_____ **5.** Mong doesn't like outdoor activities.

Test Your Vocabulary

B. Choose the word or phrase from the list that best completes each sentence.

librarian	collect	professor	free time
translate	season	hobbies	instructions
make sure	look forward to	prefer	

1. My favorite _____ is spring.

2. John wants to _____ the letter from Spanish to English.

3. We asked the _____ to help us find the book we needed.

4. This cake is easy to make. Just follow the _____ on the back of the box.

5. My father likes to _____ stamps from different countries.

6. Do you _____ coffee or tea in the morning?

7. The history _____ gives interesting lectures.

8. Her _____ are gardening and collecting stamps.

9. The children always _____ going on vacation.

10. What do you like to do in your _____?

11. He called me to _____ I got home safely.

Sharpen Your Vocabulary Skills

USING A DICTIONARY

Dictionaries are full of information that will help you learn, understand, and use English correctly. There are thousands of words in an English dictionary. To help you find the word you are looking for, the words are listed in alphabetical order. For example, in a dictionary, the word *skill* comes before the word *vocabulary* because the letter *s* comes before the letter *v* in the alphabet. When two words begin with the same letter, they are alphabetized using the second letter. *Skill* comes before *spill* because *k* comes before *p*, and *skid* comes before *skill* because *d* comes before *l*.

Alphabetizing

A. Practice your alphabetizing skills by rewriting the words in each of the following lists so that they are in alphabetical order.

1. librarian _____
   collect _____
   professor _____
   prefer _____
   instructions _____
   translate _____
   season _____

2. summer _____
   brushes _____
   information _____
   library _____
   spring _____
   future _____
   university _____

3. hobbies _____
   computer _____
   music _____
   photography _____
   garden _____
   yard _____
   calligraphy _____

4. music _____
   stereo _____
   collect _____
   garden _____
   nature _____
   flowers _____
   poetry _____

Guidewords

frugal	316		317	fun

frugal /'frugcl/ *adj* **1** careful to only buy what is necessary: *Dan's a very frugal young man.* **2** small in quantity and cost: *a frugal lunch of cheese and bread* –**frugally** *adv* –**frugality** /fru'gælcti/ *n* [U]

fruit /frut/ *n. plural* fruit or fruits **1** [C,U] the part of a plant, tree or bush that contains

equipment for frying food **2** a chicken that has been specially bred to be fried

frying pan /'.. ,./ *n* a round pan with a flat handle, used for FRYing food – see picture at PAN'

ft. the written abbreviation of FOOT.

fuchsia /'f....../ *n* **1** [U] a bright

ment. **2** the act or state of meeting a need, demand, or condition: *The offer of this contract depends upon the fulfillment of certain conditions.*

full¹ /ful/ *adj*
1 ▶CONTAINER/ROOM/PLACE◀ holding or containing as much of something, or as many things or people as possible: *Is*

reaches the ground **3 full-length play/book etc.** a play etc. of the normal length

full moon /,.'./ *n* [singular] the moon when it looks completely round.

full•ness /'fulnis/ *n* [U] in the **fullness of time** FORMAL when the right time comes: *I'm sure he'll tell us everything in the*

At the top of each dictionary page or spread of pages are two words called guidewords. Guidewords help "guide" you to the correct page. Look at the pages above. There are two guidewords: *frugal* and *fun*. The guideword *frugal* is in the left corner, and it is the first word on page 316. The guideword *fun* is in the right corner and is the last word on page 317.

> **TIP** The guideword at the left is the first word on that page. The guideword on the right is the last word on that page. Using guidewords will help you to find the word you want more quickly.

B. Use the guidewords in the boxes to put each of the following words on the appropriate dictionary page.

fuel	garbage	fuse	gash	frustrate
gaunt	gather	gadget	fulfill	galaxy
fury	gallery	gauge	gardener	fumes
funnel	gelatin	fundraising	gape	fudge
galore	gaze	furniture	fuzzy	gastric

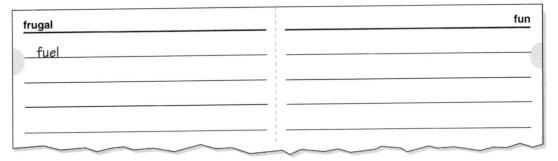

frugal	fun
fuel	

function	fuss

fuss	gambling

game	gate

gatecrash	generation gap

WORK WITH WORDS

Pronoun Reference

Pronouns are small but important words. They replace nouns. Writers often use pronouns so they won't have to repeat the same nouns over and over. Good readers look for pronouns when they read. They also look for the nouns that they refer to. This helps them read faster and understand more.

Read the paragraph again. This time notice the underlined pronouns. Each pronoun refers to a noun. Look for the noun that each pronoun replaces.

Pronouns are small but important words. <u>They</u> replace nouns. Writers often
1

use pronouns so <u>they</u> won't have to repeat the same nouns over and over.
2

Good readers look for pronouns when <u>they</u> read. <u>They</u> also look for the nouns
3   4

that <u>they</u> refer to. This helps <u>them</u> read faster and understand more.
5   6

1. They = Pronouns

2. they = Writers

3. they = Good readers

4. They = Good readers

5. they = pronouns

6. them = Good readers

Study the list of common pronouns in the chart.

he	him	his
she	her	that
it	this	
they	their	

 Pay attention to whether the pronoun is singular or plural. A singular pronoun replaces a singular noun. A plural pronoun replaces a plural noun. This will help you find the noun it refers to more easily.

Read the following sentences. Notice each underlined pronoun and look for the noun that it refers to.

1. At the library, I help students and professors find information. <u>They</u> are happy when I am able to help <u>them</u>.

   They = _____

   them = _____

2. I love to listen to classical music. <u>It</u> is my favorite kind of music.

   It = _____

3. I saved a lot of money, and I made my stereo exactly the way I wanted <u>it</u>.

   it = _____

4. Usually I write my poems in Chinese. Sometimes I translate <u>them</u> into English.

   them = _____

5. I love to take photographs of nature in different seasons of the year. I take <u>them</u> in the winter, spring, summer, and fall.

   them = _____

Sum It Up

A summary is a short statement that tells the main ideas of a longer work such as an article, interview, or book. Writing summaries will help you understand and remember what you read. Reread "Interview with Mong Meng" and complete the summary. Then compare your summary with a partner.

Mong Meng moved to the United States from _____China_____ . He enjoys
                                                          1
his job as a _____ . He has several _____ such as
                      2   3
collecting _____ , listening to classical music, gardening, doing
                    4
calligraphy, writing _____ , and _____ . Mong loves
                              5   6
books and thinks you can _____ by reading a book. He doesn't
                                    7
worry too much about the past. He thinks it's better to _____
                                                                      8
and look forward to the _____ .
                                9

Express Your Ideas

A. Discuss these questions in small groups.

1. Do you like to spend time in libraries? Why or why not?

2. Do you have a favorite kind of music? What is it? How much time do you spend listening to it?

3. It was probably difficult to build a stereo. Have you ever built or made anything that was difficult? What was it?

4. Do you agree with Mong that you can learn how to do anything from a book? Why or why not?

5. Mong likes to relax by doing calligraphy. How do you like to relax?

B. Choose one of the questions above and write a paragraph about it.

_____

_____

_____

_____

_____

Explore the Web

What is your favorite hobby? Use the Internet to find the names of some books about your favorite hobby. Use a search engine such as Google or Yahoo. Type in a few keywords like "gardening + books". Make a list of three books that you might buy about your hobby.

1. _____

2. _____

3. _____

Read Faster

Good readers are able to recognize words quickly. The following exercise will give you practice in this important reading skill.

Move your eyes as fast as you can across each row from left to right. Circle the word that is the same as the first word. Don't worry if you see a word that you don't know. Just work as fast as you can. Try to complete the exercise in thirty seconds. When you have finished, check your answers on page 155. Figure out how many answers you got right and complete the chart on page 159. This will help you see your progress.

1. might	fight	bright	light	(might)	tight	right
2. corn	horn	corner	torn	corn	born	core
3. fit	fine	five	lit	fit	fix	fist
4. stair	stain	steal	store	stale	stick	stair
5. burn	bush	turn	burn	busy	stern	learn
6. ring	thing	rings	think	sing	king	ring
7. owe	owl	out	over	owes	owe	own
8. hand	has	hat	hand	head	heat	heavy
9. pack	peak	pack	packed	pace	peace	pad
10. exit	exist	exits	expect	excel	exit	except

Have Some Fun

Work with a partner. One person is student A and uses the Student A chart on page 26. The other person is student B and uses the Student B chart on page 27. Do not look at your partner's chart. Fill in the missing pieces of information on your chart by asking your partner questions. For example, "What does Pamela do?" and "What are Pamela's hobbies?"

STUDENT A

Name	Occupation	Hobbies
Pamela	history professor	
Steve		playing tennis playing ping-pong collecting coins
Keiko	student	
Gary		fishing playing golf photography
Luis	plumber	
Vicky		gardening reading dancing
Carol	lawyer	
Mehmet		playing chess swimming painting

Name	Occupation	Hobbies
Pamela		hiking drawing playing piano
Steve	dentist	
Keiko		playing computer games bike riding playing guitar
Gary	bank manager	
Luis		painting collecting stamps jogging
Vicky	computer programmer	
Carol		going to the movies baking exercising
Mehmet	librarian	

CHAPTER 2

Look It Over
Previewing and Predicting

Look at the book cover. Discuss the questions with a partner.

1. What is the title of the book? _____

2. What do you see in the picture? _____

3. What are some examples of fast food? Why do you think those foods are

   called fast foods? _____

   _____

4. Do you like fast food? Why or why not? _____

5. Use the information—picture, title, subtitle—from the cover to make a guess about the book. What do you think it will be about? _____

> When you looked at the book cover for *Fast Food Nation*, you guessed what the book would be about. This is called predicting.

Sharpen Your Reading Skills

PREVIEWING, PREDICTING, MAKING CONNECTIONS

Before you read something, there are several things you can do to prepare yourself to read.

First, you should take a few minutes to look over the title, subtitles, cover, and then the reading itself. This is called previewing. Previewing will give you an idea about the topic of the reading and how it is organized.

Previewing means looking over a book or article quickly before you read it carefully. When you preview, look at the title and subtitle, pictures and graphics, and words in bold print or italics.

Based on what you learned from previewing, you should make guesses about what you are going to read. This is called predicting. Making guesses will keep you actively involved in reading.

Predicting is making guesses about what you are going to read. Use the information you learned from previewing and your own knowledge to make predictions about the reading.

A. Work with a partner. Follow these steps to preview the article "A Nose for the Arts" on pages 30–31.

1. Read the title and subtitle of the article. The title and subtitle usually give an idea of what the article is about.

2. Look at the pictures. Pictures, maps, and charts often show important ideas. Look at the pictures on page 30 and discuss them with your partner. Read the captions. Try to guess why the author included them.

3. The headings that are in bold print give you clues about the information in each section. Read the headings. Discuss what you think will be in each section.

4. Think about what you already know about the topic. Did you recognize anything when you previewed the article? Discuss the following questions with your partner:

    a. Have you ever seen an elephant? Where? When?

    b. What do you know about elephants?

    c. Do you think animals can learn to paint pictures or to play instruments?

5. Make some predictions. Make a list of some ideas you think might be included in the article.

    a. _____

    b. _____

    c. _____

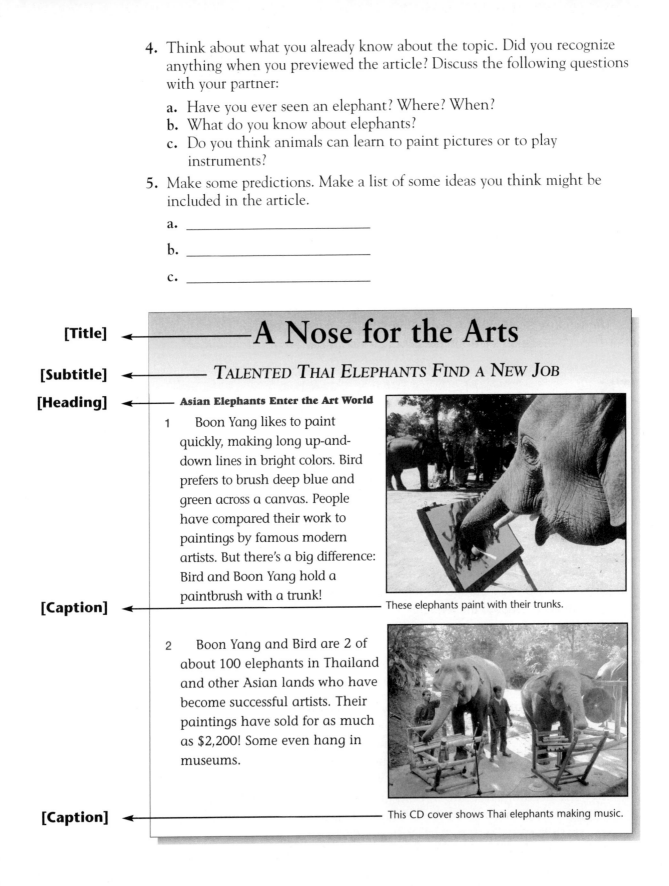

[Title] →

A Nose for the Arts

[Subtitle] →

TALENTED THAI ELEPHANTS FIND A NEW JOB

[Heading] →

Asian Elephants Enter the Art World

1   Boon Yang likes to paint quickly, making long up-and-down lines in bright colors. Bird prefers to brush deep blue and green across a canvas. People have compared their work to paintings by famous modern artists. But there's a big difference: Bird and Boon Yang hold a paintbrush with a trunk!

[Caption] →

These elephants paint with their trunks.

2   Boon Yang and Bird are 2 of about 100 elephants in Thailand and other Asian lands who have become successful artists. Their paintings have sold for as much as $2,200! Some even hang in museums.

[Caption] →

This CD cover shows Thai elephants making music.

Elephants Make Music ————————————————————→ **[Heading]**

3   Painting isn't the only kind of artwork done by Asian elephants. Some are making music too. A Thai elephant orchestra has recorded a CD. The money raised by selling CDs and paintings goes to an elephant-conservation center in Thailand.

Can Art Save Elephants? ————————————————→ **[Heading]**

4   Elephants in Thailand are in trouble. For years, they worked carrying heavy logs from rain forests. But the animals lost their jobs in 1989, when Thailand decided to protect the forests and stop logging. Some elephants wound up begging for food!

5   Artists Vitaly Komar and Alex Melamid wanted to help. They set up elephant art schools and brought attention to Thai elephants. Melamid says he's thrilled with the success of the project: "We've shown that anything is possible."

Look at your list of predictions. How many of your predictions were correct?

_____

B. Read the title of each article. Predict which ideas might be in the article. Put a check next to those ideas. Then, find a partner and compare your answers.

1. *The Internet: A Great Place to Shop*

_____ a.   You can look at lots of products very quickly.
_____ b. ways to use the Internet to research information for school work
_____ c. shopping in the comfort of your own home
_____ d. You can shop online seven days a week, twenty-four hours a day.
_____ e. comparing prices on the Internet and finding the best price for a product
_____ f. how to use a computer
_____ g. the dangers of using your credit card online

2. *Philadelphia: A City of Firsts*

_____ a. The first public library in the United States opened in Philadelphia.
_____ b. Philadelphia is the site of the first capital of the United States.
_____ c. There are many great restaurants in Philadelphia.
_____ d. *Philadelphia* is a Greek word and means "City of Brotherly Love."
_____ e. Philadelphia was home to the nation's first fire department.
_____ f. Many important "firsts" in medicine happened in Philadelphia—the first American hospital, the first medical college, and more.
_____ g. The first university in the United States, The University of Pennsylvania, opened in Philadelphia.

3. The Dos and Don'ts of Job Interviews

_____ **a.** the advantages of working part-time
_____ **b.** what to wear for a job interview
_____ **c.** arriving at interviews a few minutes early
_____ **d.** Don't be afraid to ask questions during the interview.
_____ **e.** looking for a job on the Internet
_____ **f.** answering interview questions with confidence
_____ **g.** interesting places to work

4. Saving the Planet: Every Little Bit Helps

_____ **a.** recycling glass and paper
_____ **b.** how to save water in your house
_____ **c.** buying recycled products
_____ **d.** The planets in our solar system orbit the sun.
_____ **e.** taking buses and trains to save gas
_____ **f.** turning off lights when leaving a room to save electricity
_____ **g.** eating less sugar and fat to lose weight and stay healthy

Be an Active Reader

BEFORE YOU READ

A. Work with a partner. Write your answer to each question. Then write your partner's answers. Did you have any of the same answers as your partner?

Question	Your Answer	Your Partner's Answer
What is your favorite color?		
What color clothes do you like to wear?		
What do you think is the most relaxing color?		
What color looks best on you?		

B. Join another group and discuss the questions in the chart.

C. Talk about what the people in your group are wearing. How many people are wearing the color blue? Red? Green?

Preview the Vocabulary

The words in the box are boldfaced in the article. Work with a partner and do the exercise that follows.

```
┌─────────────────────────────────────────────────┐
            Words to Watch
  loyal           uniforms          symbol
  expert          powerful          romantic
  popular         gentle
  bride           notice
└─────────────────────────────────────────────────┘
```

D. Read the following sentences. Then match the boldfaced words with the definitions below. Write the correct letter in the space provided. If you need more help, read the sentence in the article where the word appears and think about how it is used.

_____ 1. He is **loyal** to his family and friends and is always there to help them out.

_____ 2. Nurses usually wear white **uniforms**.

_____ 3. It is easy to **notice** my house. It's painted bright yellow.

_____ 4. My father studied in Japan and is an **expert** on Asian art.

_____ 5. Love and hate are **powerful** emotions.

_____ 6. A white flag is a **symbol** of peace.

_____ 7. Blue jeans are **popular** around the world.

_____ 8. My grandmother is a kind and **gentle** woman.

_____ 9. Her boyfriend gave her flowers and took her out for a **romantic** dinner.

_____ 10. The **bride** wore a beautiful wedding dress.

a. to see, feel, or hear someone or something

b. having a strong effect on someone's feelings or ideas

c. something that represents a particular quality, idea, or organization

d. never changing your feelings for a particular person, belief, or country

e. a woman at the time she gets married

f. a particular type of clothing that members of an organization or a group wear to work

g. someone with special skills or knowledge of a subject, gained as a result of training or experience

h. showing strong feelings of love

i. liked by a lot of people

j. not strong, loud, or forceful

E. Match the name of each piece of clothing with the correct picture. Write the name in the space provided.

tie   raincoat   suit   evening dress   blue jeans

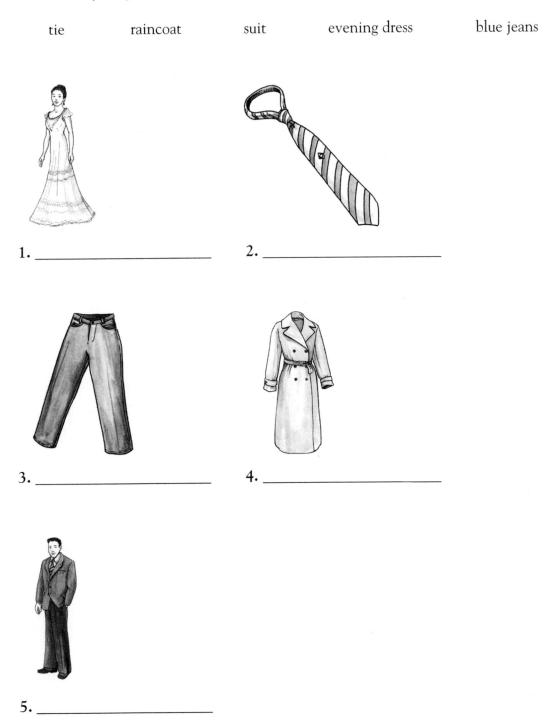

1. _____

2. _____

3. _____

4. _____

5. _____

Read with a Purpose

You are going to read an article about colors and fashions. The article talks about the special meanings of certain colors of clothes. For example, the color red can be a symbol for power. Some people wear red clothes when they want to look powerful. Before you read the article, complete the first two columns of the chart. Write what you know about colors and fashions in the first column. Write questions you would like to have answered in the second column.

What I know about colors and fashions	What I want to know about colors and fashions	What I learned about colors and fashions

As you read, answer the questions in the boxes.

What Color Are You Wearing?

The Connection between Color and Fashion

1   Do you like to wear bright colors like yellow and orange? Or, do you like to wear dark colors like black and brown? One of the first things you **notice** about a person's clothing is the color. Throughout history people have used color as **symbols**. In the past, colors had special meanings. Today the colors of clothes can have meanings too. Here are some of the ways fashion and color have connected. Since yellow and orange are easy to notice, let's see what they mean first.

Make a prediction. What do you think the next section will be about?

a. dark colors   **b.** yellow and orange   **c.** the history of color

---

Noticing Yellow and Orange

2   It is easy to notice the colors yellow and orange. Yellow and orange look happy and sunny. In ancient Rome, people wore yellow clothes to weddings. Today, some people wear yellow for safety reasons. For example, many raincoats are bright yellow. People wear yellow raincoats so other people can see them easily in the rain. Like yellow, orange can be used for safety. At night, joggers and hunters in the woods may wear orange clothes.

Was your prediction for paragraph 2 correct? Yes   No

Think about your clothes. Do you wear yellow or orange very often? Why or why not?

Make a prediction. What do you think the topic of the next section might be?

a. kinds of raincoats   **b.** the meaning of another color
c. jogging and hunting

Relax with Green

3   Green is a **gentle** color. People who work in hospitals often wear green uniforms because the color relaxes patients. Green is also the color of nature. It symbolizes growth. Many years ago in Europe, brides wore green dresses as a symbol of fertility.[1]

[1]**fertility:** *ability to have babies*

> Was your prediction for paragraph 3 correct? Yes   No
>
> Why do hospital workers wear green uniforms?

Blue Is Everywhere

4   Blue is the color of the sky and the ocean, and it is one of the most **popular** colors. Blue is also the most common color of clothes—especially since blue jeans are everywhere! The color blue shows trust and **loyalty**. Clothing **experts** tell people to wear blue to job interviews to show they will be trustworthy workers. For this same reason, U.S. police officers often wear blue **uniforms**. That way, people will trust them.

The color blue is a symbol of trust. Police officers in the United States wear blue uniforms.

The Power Color

5   Red is often considered a **powerful** color. Red ties are sometimes called power ties. Red is also a cheerful color. Some people say, "When you feel blue,[2] wear red." In China, red is the color of good luck, and people wear red to weddings. Deep red looks strong and powerful, but light red—pink—looks soft and **gentle**. Pink is a **romantic** color. It is the color of love. In the United States, pink is often associated with girls. But before the 1920s, pink was considered a boy's color.

[2]**feel blue:** *feel sad*

> Do blue or red have special meanings in your native culture? If so, what are they? Is pink associated with girls in your native culture? If not, is some other color associated with girls?

(Continued on next page.)

Royal Purple

6   Purple is the color of royalty[3] because for so long it was very expensive and hard to get. Purple dye[4] was made from snails.[5] It took more than 60,000 snails to make one pound of dye. Only very rich people could afford purple dye. Usually only kings and queens wore purple clothing.

What is the topic of the previous section?
Make a prediction. What do you think the topic of the next section might be?

Black and White Aren't Always "Black and White"

7   Black is a serious color. It is associated with death. In the West, people wear black clothes to funerals. Black clothes are also considered elegant.[6] Many people wear black clothes to formal parties. Women's evening dresses are often black. Men usually wear black suits to formal parties.

People often wear black clothes when they want to look elegant.

8   Beginning in the twentieth century, western **brides** have worn white as a symbol of goodness and happiness. In China, however, white is the color of death. Chinese people wear white clothes to funerals. White shows dirt easily; doctors and nurses wear white to show that they understand that it is important to be clean.

Is black a serious color in your country? Are any other colors considered serious?
What color do brides wear in your culture? Does white have any special meanings for you?

Conclusion

9   As you can see, a colorful world is a world of meaning because people have always used colors as symbols. Look around and you will notice the many ways that fashion and color have connected.

AFTER YOU READ

Fill in the third column in the chart on page 35. Did the article answer any of your questions from the second column? Which ones? Look at the things you wrote in the first column. Were any of your ideas confirmed or rejected in the article? Which ones?

[3] **royalty:** members of a royal family, such as kings and queens

[4] **dye:** a substance you use to change the color of hair or clothes

[5]

[6] **elegant:** very beautiful and graceful

Check Your Comprehension

A. Choose the word or phrase that best completes each sentence. Circle the letter.

1. The color white is a sign of death in _____.
   a. the United States
   b. China
   c. Rome

2. _____ is a popular color in hospitals because it relaxes people.
   a. Green
   b. Yellow
   c. Pink

3. _____ is a serious color.
   a. Red
   b. Black
   c. Green

4. Police officers wear blue to show they are _____
   a. loyal
   b. romantic
   c. clean

5. People wear the color _____ for safety.
   a. red
   b. green
   c. yellow

6. The color _____ used to be expensive and hard to get.
   a. white
   b. purple
   c. blue

7. The color _____ is a symbol of growth.
   a. white
   b. green
   c. blue

8. In the past, boys wore _____, but now it is often considered a girl's color.
   a. pink
   b. yellow
   c. blue

Test Your Vocabulary

B. Choose the word from the list that best completes each sentence.

loyal	uniforms	symbols
expert	powerful	romantic
popular	gentle	
bride	notice	

1. Soldiers in the army wear _____.

2. Did you _____ her new red shoes?

3. Ruth is a _____ friend. I can always trust her.

4. Hate can be a dangerous and _____ feeling.

5. She knows a lot about art, and she is an _____ on Egyptian art.

6. The fifty stars on the American flag are _____ of the fifty states.

7. Pizza is one of the most _____ foods among college students.

8. The _____ looks beautiful in her long white dress.

9. I love Valentine's Day. It's such a _____ holiday.

10. Please use a soft and _____ voice when you talk to my baby.

Sharpen Your Vocabulary Skills

USING A DICTIONARY

Each word defined in the dictionary is called an entry word. Look at the dictionary entry for *suit*. The entry shows you how to spell and pronounce the word. It also tells you the meaning of a word. One of the most important reasons you use a dictionary is to learn the meaning of a word. Since many words in English have more than one meaning, the dictionary lists all of the meanings.

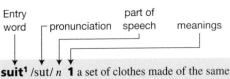

Entry word | pronunciation | part of speech | meanings

suit¹ /sut/ *n* **1** a set of clothes made of the same material, including a short coat with pants or a skirt: *a dark gray suit* **2** a piece or pieces of clothing used for a special purpose: *a swimming suit* **3** [C, U] ⇨ LAWSUIT: *A homeowner **filed suit against** the country and lost.* **4** one of the four types of cards in a set of playing cards

As you can see, the dictionary numbers and lists all of the meanings. Look again at the dictionary entry for *suit*. The dictionary lists four meanings for *suit*.

A. Use the dictionary entry for *suit* to look up the meaning of *suit* in each sentence. Write the definition that best fits the meaning of the sentence.

1. Mr. Simmons filed a <u>suit</u> against the company.

   _____

2. John wore his dark gray <u>suit</u> to the wedding.

   _____

3. A deck of cards has four <u>suits</u>: spades, hearts, clubs, and diamonds.

   _____

4. Patty is going to wear her new diving <u>suit</u> when she goes deep-sea diving.

   _____

B. Use the dictionary entry for *tie* to look up the meaning of *tie* in each sentence. Write the definition that best fits the meaning of the sentence.

> **tie**^{2} *n* **1** a long narrow piece of cloth that men wear around their neck, tied in a knot outside their shirts **2** a relationship between two people, groups, or countries: *close family ties* **3** a piece of string, wire etc. used in order to fasten or close something such as a bag **4** the result of a game, competition, or election in which two or more people get the same number of points, votes etc.: *The game **ended in a tie.***

1. The score of the basketball game was 33 to 33. It ended in a <u>tie</u>.

   _____

2. There are close economic <u>ties</u> between the United States and Canada.

   _____

3. Mr. Davis wore his blue <u>tie</u> to a job interview.

   _____

4. Please close that bag with a <u>tie</u>.

   _____

WORK WITH WORDS

Synonyms and Antonyms

A good way to expand your vocabulary and help you remember new words is by learning synonyms and antonyms.

> A **synonym** is a word that has the same meaning or almost the same meaning as another word. For example, *mad* is a synonym of *angry*. An **antonym** is a word that has the opposite meaning of another word. For example, *war* is an antonym of *peace*.

A. Write an S if the words are synonyms. Write an A if the words are antonyms. Use your dictionary to look up the meanings of unfamiliar words.

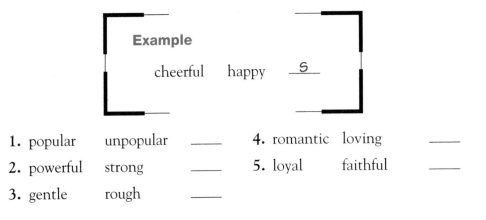

Example

cheerful   happy   _S_

1. popular   unpopular   _____
2. powerful   strong   _____
3. gentle   rough   _____
4. romantic   loving   _____
5. loyal   faithful   _____

Pronoun Reference

B. Read the following sentences. Notice each underlined pronoun and look for the noun that it refers to.

1. Since yellow and orange are easy to notice, let's see what <u>they</u> mean first.

   they = _____

2. Green is also the color of nature. <u>It</u> symbolizes growth.

   It = _____

3. For this same reason, U.S. police officers often wear blue uniforms. That way, people will trust <u>them</u>.

   them = _____

4. Pink is a romantic color. <u>It</u> is the color of love.

   It = _____

5. White shows dirt easily; doctors and nurses wear white to show that <u>they</u> understand that it is important to be clean.

   they = _____

Sum It Up

Reread "What Color Are You Wearing?" and complete the summary.

The colors of ___clothes___ are often used as symbols. For example, the color
          1

_____ is a symbol for loyalty. Experts advise people to wear blue to
  2

_____ to show they will be _____. U.S. police officers also often
  3   4

wear blue _____. Another example is the color _____, which
          5   6

means _____.
      7

Express Your Ideas

A. Discuss these questions in small groups.

1. Are the majority of your clothes the same color? If yes, what color? Why?

2. Do you agree that you can use color to change your mood? Why or why not?

3. Do you care what color your room is painted? Why or why not?

4. The article talks about some colors that have different meaning in different parts of the world. Compare the meaning of colors in your native culture with their meaning in your classmates' native cultures.

5. In English, we have many expressions that use colors. For example, if someone is really angry, we say "he is seeing red." If someone is sad, we say "she's blue." Can you think of expressions in your native language that use colors?

B. Choose one of the questions above and write a paragraph about it.

_____

_____

_____

_____

_____

_____

Explore the Web

1. As you know, colors mean different things in different countries. Choose a color and explore the Web to find out what it means in three different countries. Use keywords such as "white + meaning + Japan."

2. Find a partner who chose the same color but researched its meaning in another country. Compare your information and then complete the chart below.

Color	Country	Meaning

Read Faster

Move your eyes as fast as you can across each row from left to right. Circle the word that is the same as the first word. Don't worry if you see a word that you don't know. Just work as fast as you can. Try to complete the exercise in thirty seconds. When you have finished, check your answers on page 155. Figure out how many answers you got right and complete the chart on page 159. This will help you see your progress.

1.	near	nearly	next	nest	never	nearer	near
2.	law	lax	lawn	law	raw	late	rate
3.	pick	tick	trick	pack	picky	pickle	pick
4.	dish	dish	disk	dirt	fish	fast	dishes
5.	fear	feet	ear	tear	gear	fear	feel
6.	pie	lie	pie	peace	pit	pick	tie
7.	tall	talk	tail	ten	tell	tan	tall
8.	eye	end	oil	eight	eyes	eye	eight
9.	mix	milk	mock	model	fix	mix	mixed
10.	have	had	heaven	heavy	have	hats	head

Have Some Fun

Complete the puzzle using the clues provided.

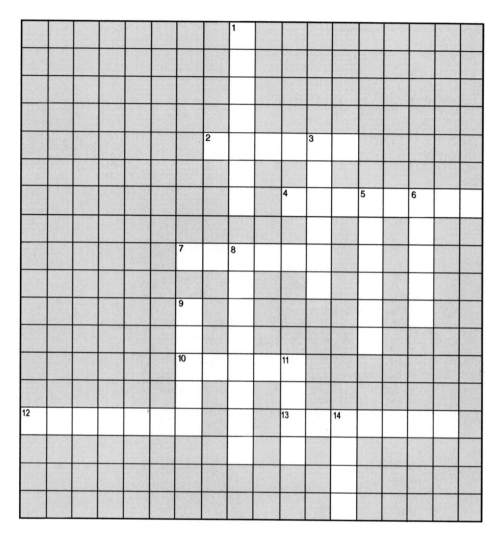

Across

2. Joggers often wear the color ___.
4. Police officers often wear blue ___.
7. Something that represents something else is a ___.
10. In China, ___ is the color of death.
12. Blue is one of the most ___ colors.
13. Black is a ___ color.

Down

1. Clothing ___ say that blue shows you are loyal.
3. Pink looks soft and ___.
5. Black is often worn to ___ parties.
6. Green helps people to ___.
8. Colors often have special ___.
9. Deep red is a color that shows ___.
11. Yellow and orange are ___ to notice.
14. In the past, only ___ people could afford purple.

CHAPTER 3

Read for Meaning
Main Ideas and Supporting Details

Look at the picture. Discuss what you see with a partner. Then answer the questions.

1. What is the most important idea in the picture?

   a. The clown is wearing a hat.
   b. The people are at a circus performance.

2. What things in the picture describe or give information about the main idea? Make a list. You may need to use a dictionary.

Example

The people are at a circus performance.

_____

_____

_____

_____

_____

When you identified the most important idea in the picture as "b. The people are at a circus performance," you found the main idea. When you looked at the things that gave you more information about the man, you found supporting details. You should also look for main ideas and supporting details as you read. Knowing both the main idea and details will help you understand and remember what you read.

Sharpen Your Reading Skills

MAIN IDEAS

You know that good readers look for the topic of what they are reading. Good readers also look for the main idea. The **main idea** is the writer's most important point about the topic.

> To find the main idea of a paragraph, ask yourself, "What does the author want me to know about the topic?"

How Do You Find the Main Idea of a Paragraph?

In order to find the main idea of a paragraph, first you need to find the topic. Then you need to ask yourself, "What does the author want me to know about the topic?" The answer is the main idea. Many times you will find the answer in one sentence. This is called the **topic sentence**. The topic sentence states the main idea of the paragraph. The topic sentence is often the first sentence of a paragraph, but sometimes it is the last sentence or a sentence in the middle of the paragraph.

A. Read the paragraphs. Find the topic of each paragraph. Then underline the sentence that tells the main idea.

Example

The Dutch painter Rembrandt van Rijn (1606–1669) was one of the most famous artists of all time. He painted 650 oil paintings. In addition, he drew over 2,000 pictures. Rembrandt is best known for his paintings of people who lived in Amsterdam. *The Night Watch* is one of his most popular paintings.

Topic: <u>Rembrandt</u>

1. Camping is a wonderful way to spend a vacation. First of all, it doesn't cost very much money. Instead of paying for a hotel, you can stay at a campsite in a state park or national forest. Most campgrounds are located in beautiful places with lakes, rivers, or mountains. You can take walks through a forest, climb up a mountain, or swim in a river. Sleeping inside a tent and cooking over a campfire can be lots of fun. Children especially like to go camping, but people of all ages who love nature and the outdoors will enjoy camping.

   Topic: _____

2. Eating in a fast-food restaurant is fast and easy, but it's not always good for you. For one thing, the food you eat in fast-food restaurants has a lot of fat. Fast food also has too much salt. Another problem is that the amount of food in each serving is often large in fast-food restaurants, so it's easy to eat too much. Finally, there are usually not many fruits or vegetables on the menu in a fast-food restaurant. Next time you eat in a fast-food restaurant, think about what you are eating and how much you are eating.

   Topic: _____

3. Every day millions of people in cities ride subways to get from one place to another. Subways can take people places faster than cars or buses because they do not go on busy streets. Today there are over sixty subway systems in cities around the world. The best-known subways are in London, New York, Moscow, and Paris. New York has the busiest subway system, and Moscow has the largest.

   Topic: _____

4.   Are you thinking about buying a digital camera? It might be a good idea. When you use a digital camera, you don't have to buy film or pay to have your pictures developed. If you have a computer you can print the pictures yourself at home. In addition, when you use a digital camera, you can change and improve your pictures. It is easy to cut out bad parts or to make the photos lighter, darker, bigger, or smaller. Finally, digital photography is fun. It is so easy to send digital photos to family and friends using e-mail. As you can see, there are many reasons to use digital photography.

Topic: _____

SUPPORTING DETAILS

As you know, the sentences in a paragraph are all about one topic. Together they develop one main idea. To help you understand the main idea, the writer adds supporting details. The **supporting details** give more information about the topic. They are not as general as the main idea. After you identify the topic and the main idea, you should look for details that support it.

B. Look at the photograph of a dog. Discuss what you see with a partner. What details does the artist use to show you that the dog is dressed to go out? Make a list. Compare your list with a partner.

Example

the dog is carrying bags

_____

_____

_____

_____

Supporting details can be examples, facts, or reasons. Supporting details help you understand more about the main idea. They tell who, what, when, where, why, how, how much, or how many.

c. One sentence in each group below is the main idea. The other sentences are supporting details. Write MI in front of the main idea and SD in front of the details.

Example

_SD_ For example, in the United States the color white means goodness, but in China white means death.

_MI_ Colors have different meanings in different countries.

_SD_ Red represents death in Egypt, but in China, red is good luck.

1.
____ It also provided them with work.
____ The Nile River was very important to the people of ancient Egypt.
____ It gave them good farmland for food.

2.
____ The Grand Canyon is 1 mile (2 km) deep and 300 miles (482 km) long.
____ Every year an average of 5 million people visit the Grand Canyon.
____ The Grand Canyon is one of the great natural wonders of the world.

3.
____ Robert Hooke was an outstanding scientist and inventor.
____ One of Hooke's most important inventions was a new kind of microscope.
____ He did many valuable experiments at the Royal Society in London.

4.
____ All the schools and businesses were closed for two days.
____ The roads were so slippery that there were many accidents.
____ The snowstorm caused our city many problems.

5.
____ My roommate, Jack, and I are not compatible.
____ I am a neat and organized person, but Jack is messy.
____ Jack stays up late listening to loud music, but I prefer to go to sleep early.

6.
____ Trees give us wood.
____ They give us oxygen to breathe.
____ Trees do many important things.

7.

_____ We call my younger sister Su Su.

_____ My grandparents' nicknames are Pops and Mi Mi.

_____ My nickname is Jud, and my brother's is Buddy.

_____ Everyone in my family has a nickname.

8.

_____ There is a supermarket on the next block.

_____ It's easy to find a parking space near my apartment.

_____ My apartment is in a great location.

_____ The neighborhood is safe and clean.

D. Read the following paragraphs. Identify the main idea and write it in the space provided. Then make a list of the details that support the main idea.

Example

    My cousins live all over the United States. My cousin Jim and his family live in Texas. Sally and Carl live in Rhode Island. Marianne, Nicole, and Francine are in college in the East now, so they don't live at home in Kansas anymore. Although we are spread out all over the country, we communicate often by e-mail.

Main Idea: My cousins live all over the United States.

Supporting Details: Sally and Carl live in Rhode Island.

                         Nicole and Francine are in college in the East now.

                         We communicate often by e-mail.

1.   Roberta has lots of hobbies that keep her busy in her free time. She likes to ski in the winter and play golf in the summer. Roberta plays the piano, and she is taking lessons to learn to play the guitar. She likes to draw cartoons and is a pretty good artist. She also loves to cook and read cookbooks. With all these hobbies, Roberta is always busy.

Main Idea: _____

Supporting Details: _____

                _____

                _____

                _____

                _____

2.   Ivan wants to quit smoking for many reasons. First of all, cigarettes are expensive, so he can save money if he stops smoking. Second, his girlfriend doesn't like the smell of cigarettes, and he wants to make her happy. The most important reason to quit smoking is because of his health. Everyone knows that smoking is unhealthy and can cause serious diseases like cancer. For all of these reasons, Ivan is trying hard to find a way to quit smoking.

Main Idea: _____

Supporting Details: _____

_____

_____

_____

_____

3.   My grandmother was a wonderful woman who gave her family good advice. She taught us to work hard at home and in school. We always had to help with the housework, so we learned how to cook, clean, and take care of the house. My grandmother also expected us to study hard in school because she wanted us to succeed in life. Most importantly, she taught us to respect ourselves and to respect other people. I will always remember the lessons I learned from my grandmother.

Main Idea: _____

Supporting Details: _____

_____

_____

_____

_____

4.   Americans spend a lot of money on their pets, especially cats and dogs. Supermarkets offer many kinds of expensive pet food and toys for animals. There are also special beauty shops for pets to get a shampoo and haircut. There are even pet psychiatrists for animals with psychological problems. There seems to be no limit to what Americans will do for their pets.

Main Idea: _____

Supporting Details: _____

_____

_____

_____

_____

Be an Active Reader

BEFORE YOU READ

A. When do you take photographs? Put a check next to the times you usually take pictures. Then discuss your answers with a partner.

☐ at birthday parties   ☐ on trips to other places

☐ at weddings   ☐ at graduations

☐ on vacations   ☐ at sports events

☐ on holidays   ☐ Other: _____

B. Where do you keep your photographs? Put a check next to those places. Then discuss your answers with a partner.

☐ in a photo album   ☐ in your wallet   ☐ in a box

☐ in frames   ☐ in a drawer   Other: _____

C. There is an old saying that "a picture is worth a thousand words." What do you think this saying means? Do you agree with it?

Preview the Vocabulary

The words and word phrases in the box are boldfaced in the article. Work with a partner and do the exercise that follows.

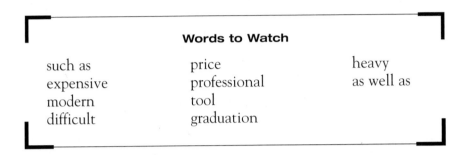

Words to Watch

such as	price	heavy
expensive	professional	as well as
modern	tool	
difficult	graduation	

D. Read the following sentences. Then match the boldfaced words and phrases with the definitions below. Write the correct letter in the space provided. If you need more help, read the sentence in the article where the word appears and think about how it is used.

_____ **1.** I like winter sports **such as** skiing and ice-skating.
_____ **2.** This is a **difficult** math problem. I can't do it.
_____ **3.** We took lots of pictures at my brother's **graduation** from high school.
_____ **4.** The **price** of this book is $15.00.
_____ **5.** This box is too **heavy**. I can't move it by myself.
_____ **6.** That car is $5,000 more than all of the others. It's too **expensive**.
_____ **7.** My uncle has a job doing something he loves. He's a **professional** basketball player.
_____ **8.** He ate two slices of pizza, **as well as** a plate of spaghetti.
_____ **9.** **Modern** computers are much faster than older ones.
_____ **10.** Computers are an important **tool** for scientists.

a. not easy to do or understand
b. in addition to something else
c. belonging to the present time or the most recent time
d. weighing a lot
e. something, such as a piece of equipment, that is useful for a particular purpose
f. a ceremony at which you receive a degree or diploma
g. costing a lot of money
h. for example
i. the amount of money that must be paid in order to buy something
j. doing a job, sport, or activity for money

E. Match the name of the item with the correct picture. Write the word under the correct picture.

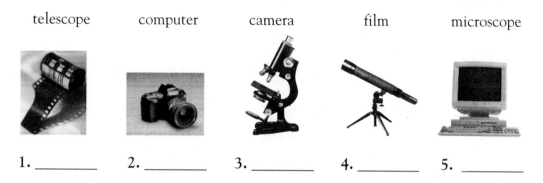

| telescope | computer | camera | film | microscope |

1. _____ 2. _____ 3. _____ 4. _____ 5. _____

Read with a Purpose

You are going to read an article about photography. The article talks about many aspects of photography such as the history of photography and the uses of photography. Before you read the article, complete the first two columns of the chart.

What I know about photography	What I want to know about photography	What I learned about photography

As you read the article, complete the chart on pages 57–58.

Picture This: Photography Past and Present

Introduction

1   A photograph is something everyone can understand. It does not matter what language you speak or what country you come from; a photograph tells a story without words. Do you know where the word *photography* comes from? It comes from two Greek words: *photo* for "drawing" and *graphien* for "light." Together the two words mean "drawing with light." When you take a photograph, rays of light make a picture on the film inside a camera.

Photography in Our Everyday Lives

2   We use photography in many ways in our everyday lives. People all over the world take pictures of their family and friends. Some take pictures on special occasions **such as** birthdays, weddings, and **graduations**. Parents often take pictures of their children at sports events or musical performances. Lots of people take photographs when they are traveling or on vacation. They keep the pictures so that they can remember their trips. Photos are a great way to help us remember important times in our lives.

The Power of Photography

3   Photographs are powerful **tools**. They can teach us about people and places in other parts of the world. They also help us record special moments in history such as the first landing on the moon. Photography is important to doctors and scientists too. Cameras can go places where we cannot go and see things that we cannot see with just our eyes. For example, doctors use a small camera attached to a microscope to see inside the human body. Scientists use tiny cameras attached to a telescope to see things far away in space. Photography is also a powerful tool in business. Businesses use photographs to

help sell their products and services. As you can see, photographs can teach us new things, record information, and even sell products.

The Birth of Modern Photography

4   **Modern** photography was invented in the early twentieth century. In the 1800s only a few people knew how to take photographs. Cameras back then were large, **heavy, expensive**, and **difficult** to use. Therefore, most people who took photographs were **professional** photographers. How did things change? In 1900, a man named George Eastman invented a small camera. The new camera was so easy to use that almost anyone could take pictures with it. Eastman called his new camera the Kodak Brownie. Kodak Brownies were inexpensive **as well as** easy to use. The **price** of a Brownie was just one dollar. Soon thousands of people were buying Kodak Brownies and taking pictures.

New Developments

5   The technology of photography continues to develop. The biggest development involves the use of computers and digital cameras. Digital photography is a way to make pictures without using film. Digital photographs can be printed out on a computer. With digital photography, you can make changes to your pictures. You can change the colors or sizes of your photos. You can also take out the parts of the picture that you don't like.

Conclusion

6   Today, taking pictures is so easy that almost anyone can try to be a photographer. Photography is something that can be personal and it can be professional. It can be scientific and it can be for business. No matter what it is used for, photography plays a major role in all of our lives.

Picture This: Photography Past and Present

Paragraph 2

Topic: _____

Main Idea: We use photography in many ways in our everyday lives.

Supporting Details:

1. _____

2. _____

3. _____

(Continued on next page.)

<u>Paragraph 3</u>

Topic: _____

Main Idea: _____ .

Supporting Details:

1. <u>Photographs can teach us about people and places in other parts of the world.</u>

2. _____ .

3. _____ .

4. _____ .

5. _____ .

<u>Paragraph 4</u>

Topic: _____

Main Idea: _____ .

Supporting Details:

1. <u>In 1900, George Eastman invented a new, small camera.</u>

2. _____ .

3. _____ .

<u>Paragraph 5</u>

Topic: _____

Main Idea: <u>The technology of photography continues to develop.</u>

Supporting Details:

1. _____ .

2. _____ .

3. _____ .

AFTER YOU READ

Fill in the third column of the chart on page 55. Did the article answer any of your questions from the second column? Which ones? Look at the things you wrote in the first column. Were any of your ideas confirmed or rejected in the article? Which ones?

Check Your Comprehension

A. True or False? Write T (True) or F (False) next to each statement.

_____ **1.** Photographs help us record special moments in history.

_____ **2.** In the 1800s many people knew how to take photographs.

_____ **3.** The word *photography* comes from a Latin word.

_____ **4.** George Eastman invented a small camera.

_____ **5.** Digital photography doesn't use film.

_____ **6.** Photography has stayed the same since the early 1900s.

Test Your Vocabulary

B. Choose the word or phrase from the list that best completes each sentence.

> such as   difficult   heavy
> tool   price   as well as
> expensive   professional
> modern   graduation

1. I can't afford to buy an _____ stereo. It costs too much money.

2. You won't be able to carry that suitcase. It's very _____.

3. Many lives are saved because of advances in _____ medicine.

4. Can television be used as a _____ for learning?

5. My son hopes to make a lot of money as a _____ tennis player.

6. Don't worry. This computer is not _____ to use.

7. He has a home in Ottawa _____ an apartment in Toronto.

8. My parents took lots of pictures at my college _____.

9. I like shopping in big cities _____ Tokyo, Paris, and New York.

10. Can you tell me the _____ of this sweater?

Sharpen Your Vocabulary Skills

USING A DICTIONARY

The dictionary tells you the part of speech of each word. Knowing the part of speech will help you learn to use a word correctly. The parts of speech are abbreviated as follows: n. = noun, v. = verb, adj. = adjective, adv. = adverb.

A. Use your dictionary to identify the part of speech of each underlined word.

> **Example**
>
> Photographs are <u>powerful</u> tools.
>
> Part of speech: <u>adjective</u>

1. In 1884, a man named George Eastman <u>invented</u> a small camera.

   Part of speech: _____

2. Businesses around the world <u>often</u> use photographs to help sell their products and services.

   Part of speech: _____

3. Scientists use <u>tiny</u> cameras attached to a telescope to see things far away in space.

   Part of speech: _____

4. They also help us record <u>special</u> moments in history such as the first landing on the moon.

   Part of speech: _____

5. In 1905 he opened a <u>gallery</u> that showed the photographs of different artists.

   Part of speech: _____

Some words can be used as more than one part of speech. For those words, the part of speech used most often is usually listed first. When you look up a word, first determine the part of speech. Then look for the meaning that fits best in the sentence you have read.

major¹ /ˈmeɪdʒə / *adj* very large or important, especially when compared to other things or people of similar kind: *The car needs major repairs. A major operation* DONT SAY "major than" SAY "more important than" or "bigger than"— compare MINOR'

major² *n* **1** the main subject that you study at a college or university: *His major is history.* — compare MINOR² **2** also **Major** an officer who has a middle rank in the Army, Air Force, or Marines

major³ *v*

major in sth *phr v* [T] to study something as your main subject at a college or university: *I'm majoring in biology.*

B. Look at the dictionary entry above to determine the part of speech of *major* in each of the following sentences. Then write the correct definition.

Example

No matter what it is used for, photography plays a <u>major</u> role in all of our lives.

Part of speech: <u>adjective</u>

Definition: <u>very large or important, especially when compared to other things or people of a similar kind</u>

---

1. Joanne <u>is majoring</u> in chemistry in college and then plans to go to medical school.

   Part of speech: _____

   Definition: _____

2. My uncle is a <u>major</u> in the army.

   Part of speech: _____

   Definition: _____

3. This plan is terrible. We need to make some <u>major</u> changes.

   Part of speech: _____

   Definition: _____

4. My <u>major</u> is history, but I am also interested in English literature.

   Part of speech: _____

   Definition: _____

C. Use a dictionary to determine the part of speech of *record* in each of the following sentences. Then write the correct definition.

1. They also help us <u>record</u> special moments in history such as the first landing on the moon.

   Part of speech: _____

   Definition: _____

2. Jason broke the <u>record</u> for the fastest swimmer in our school.

   Part of speech: _____

   Definition: _____

3. Some people like to collect old <u>records</u> from their favorite musical groups.

   Part of speech: _____

   Definition: _____

4. I keep a <u>record</u> of all the money I spend on food and entertainment each month.

   Part of speech: _____

   Definition: _____

5. She <u>recorded</u> her first song ten years ago.

   Part of speech: _____

   Definition: _____

WORK WITH WORDS

Word Families

Many words in English change their form when they change their part of speech. Words might have noun, verb, adjective, and adverb forms. The different forms of a word make up a word family. Look at the chart below. It shows some common word families. Learning the different words in a word family will help you increase your vocabulary.

Noun	Verb	Adjective
photo/photograph/ photography	photograph	photographic
information	inform	informative
invention	invent	inventive
creation	create	creative

A. Complete the following sentences with the correct word from the chart. Be sure to use the correct form of the word.

1. Your teacher will _____ you of your grade.

2. My sister is an artist. She is very _____ .

3. The Kodak Brownie was a great _____ .

4. I keep all of my _____ in an album.

5. You can find a lot of _____ about words in a dictionary.

6. Do you know who _____ the microscope?

Pronoun Reference

B. Read the following sentences. Notice each underlined pronoun and write the noun that it refers to.

1. Do you know where the word *photography* comes from? <u>It</u> comes from two Greek words: *photo* for "drawing" and *graphien* for "light."

   It = _____

2. Photographs are powerful tools. <u>They</u> can teach us about people and places in other parts of the world. <u>They</u> also help us record special moments in history such as the first landing on the moon.

   They = _____
   They = _____

3. Eastman called <u>his</u> new camera the Kodak Brownie.

   his = _____

4. The new camera was so easy to use that almost anyone could take pictures with <u>it</u>.

   it = _____

5. Photography is something that can be personal and professional. <u>It</u> can be scientific and <u>it</u> can be artistic.

   It = _____
   it = _____

Synonyms and Antonyms

C. Write an S if the words are synonyms. Write an A if the words are antonyms. Use your dictionary to look up the meanings of unfamiliar words.

1. expensive   costly   _____

2. heavy   light   _____

3. difficult   easy   _____

4. modern   old   _____

5. professional   amateur   _____

Sum It Up

Reread "Picture This: Photography Past and Present" and complete the summary.

Photography is part of our everyday lives in many ways. For example, people take pictures of their _____ and friends at _____, _____, and _____. Photographs are also powerful tools. For example, photography is used by _____, _____, and _____. The birth of modern photography began in _____ when George Eastman _____ a new camera, called the _____. Before that photography was for _____. But with the invention of _____, less expensive cameras, anyone could take pictures. Recent developments in photography have also created big changes. The digital camera allows people to make pictures without using _____. In addition, with a digital camera, people can _____ and _____ their photos themselves.

Express Your Ideas

A. Discuss these questions in small groups.

1. Do you like to take pictures? If yes, do you usually take pictures of people, events, or places?
2. Do you prefer to take photos in black and white or in color? Why?
3. Do you own a digital camera? If yes, do you edit and print your own photos?
4. Have you ever gone to a photography exhibition at a museum?
5. Do you agree that photography is an art form? Why or why not?

B. Choose one of the questions above and write a paragraph about it.

_____

_____

_____

_____

_____

Explore the Web

A. Work with a partner. Choose a famous photographer from the list below and explore the Web to look at some of his or her photographs. Choose one photograph that you like and print it out.

Adams, Ansel	Altman, Robert	Avedon, Richard
Dennis, Nigel	Ferro, Jean	La Chapelle, David
Leibowitz, Annie	Mark, Mary Ellen	Salicki, Roman

B. Share your photograph with your classmates. Then, with the class, discuss all of the photographs and decide which one the class thinks is the most interesting.

Read Faster

Move your eyes as fast as you can across each row from left to right. Circle the word that is the same as the first word. Don't worry if you see a word that you don't know. Just work as fast as you can. Try to complete the exercise in thirty seconds. When you have finished, check your answers on page 156. Figure out how many answers you got right and complete the chart on page 159. This will help you see your progress.

1.	pint	pine	pinch	pin	pint	pile	pike
2.	deep	deem	deal	deed	deepen	deep	deeply
3.	cameo	camera	calm	camp	came	campus	cameo
4.	does	does	don't	dean	deep	doll	donut
5.	teeth	tooth	tool	team	teeth	teal	time
6.	said	sake	sail	say	sad	said	sale
7.	book	boor	boot	boat	boom	books	book
8.	license	silence	liver	license	sliver	slice	lichen
9.	dessert	desert	despot	destroy	dessert	destiny	distinct
10.	laugh	laud	launch	launder	laughter	laundry	laugh

Have Some Fun

Find the fifteen words related to photography on the opposite page and circle them. The words may be horizontal, vertical, diagonal, and backwards. One word has been found for you.

ADVERTISING	FRAME	PHOTOGRAPHY
CAMERA	HOBBY	PICTURE
DIGITAL	MEDICINE	PRINT
EDIT	PERSONAL	PROFESSIONAL
FILM	PHOTO	SCIENCE

Q R C A Z X K Q O V E I L X L Z N Y A S
D V Q G D R B K W G C L J A U F N R Z V
I K G R A V A S N Z N Q N J K A S A A Y
D K C E I Q E M B Q E O T B U H R H D H Z
I Z M L B R X R R F I G O S B X F H Y P
C W S A A D H L T S C S G M H Y Q K M O
F P N D W T G S S I S B P M T Y D K M L
X N I U Q N U E A G S Y I H U J V T D P
U D H M L M F M J O B I H R T N Z Q B L
E P H O T O G R A P H Y N M M P A O Z R
T O V E R U T C I P T U E G P R H Y L L
L Q W P M L I F K C E D D I E L O O G R
N A Q M N L S A F B I C L M R N B N T P
P T T J O E P W Y C R H A H S J B P R O
L L I I H X G T I C F C N C O G Y I Q I
V N S D G O G N B U L L F O N T N X X M
J J O Q E I E L M T T P X B A T D P N M
G F Y T H Z D H Z A Q E W Y L Q D N T Z
W G Y I F D R I D Z V W L R I P Q D X C
T B Q V A A R E X Y F R A M E W X O R I

CHAPTER 4

Find the Order
Recognizing Time Order

Soure: PEANUTS reprinted by persmission of United Features Syndicate, Inc.

Look at the pictures. They are all from one comic strip, but they are not in the right order. When you put the pictures in the right order, they will tell a story. It is about a dog and his secretary. The secretary is a bird. The dog is always having problems with his secretary. Today his secretary is late getting back to work.

1. Think about the pictures from the cartoon. Discuss the pictures with a partner and number them 1–4 in the space provided, so they tell the story in the right order.
2. Join another group and compare your order.
3. What clues did you use to help you put the pictures in order?

When you decided which picture came first, second, third, and so on, you thought about the order of events in the story. In the same way, you often need to think about the order of events when you read.

Sharpen Your Reading Skills

RECOGNIZING TIME ORDER

Most stories, cartoons, letters, and articles are organized according to some kind of order. Understanding the order of a reading will help you read it more easily. One of the most common types of order is called time order. When a reading is organized by time order, the writer tells you what happened first, second, third, and so on. In this chapter you will practice recognizing time order.

As you read, look for clues that give you information about the order of events. Dates and times can help you understand the order of events. Other clues are signal words that a writer uses to explain the order of events. Here are some common signal words of time order.

after	finally	later	then
at last	first	next	when
before	last	second	while

A. Look at the pictures on the next page. They tell you how to remove a water mark on a wooden table. Choose the sentence below that describes each picture and write it on the lines under the picture.

Lay the towel on the white water mark.
Check the stain. The stain should be gone.
Leave the mayonnaise on the stain for about fifteen minutes.
Spread about 2 tablespoons of mayonnaise on a paper towel.
Press the paper towel lightly with your fingers.

How to Remove a Water Mark from a Wooden Table

_____

_____

_____

_____

_____

B.   Complete the paragraph.

Did you ever leave a glass of water on a wooden table? If so, you may find a

white mark on the table. Don't worry. It is easy to remove the water mark if you

follow the steps in these pictures. _____, you

1

need to spread about 2 tablespoons of mayonnaise on a paper towel. Then,

_____. After that, _____.

2   3

Remember to _____. Finally, _____.

4   5

C.   Read the paragraphs. Think about the order of events in each one. Then, number
the sentences that follow each paragraph so they are in the correct time order.

Example

Yesterday was a terrible day for Maggie. She woke up late because her alarm
clock didn't ring. Then, she couldn't find her car keys and spent fifteen minutes
looking for them. When Maggie arrived at her college, she couldn't find a
parking space on campus. She had to park three blocks away. The teacher
looked angry when Maggie walked into class late. The teacher was giving the
class a surprise test with difficult questions. Finally, on the way home from
school, Maggie's car got a flat tire. Maggie hopes tomorrow will be a better day.

  2   Maggie couldn't find her car keys.

  4   Maggie's car had a flat tire.

  1   Maggie woke up late.

  3   Maggie couldn't find a parking space on campus.

1.   There was a fox who was very hungry. He was looking for something to eat.
He saw a crow fly up into a tree with a piece of cheese in her mouth. The fox
wanted the cheese for himself. The fox thought for a minute. Then he said to
the crow, "You are very beautiful. Your feathers are shiny and your eyes are
bright. Is your voice beautiful too? Will you sing a song for me?" The crow was
pleased because the fox had praised her, and she began to sing. Naturally the
cheese fell out of the crow's mouth and into the mouth of the fox. The fox ate
the cheese and said to the fox, "Do not trust people who praise you too much."

_____ The fox told the crow that she was beautiful and asked her to sing.

_____ The crow began to sing.

_____ The cheese fell out of the crow's mouth and into the fox's mouth.

_____ A hungry fox saw a crow with some cheese.

2. When Janine graduated from college, she moved to New York City. At first she hated New York because the city was so big. She also felt lonely since she didn't know anyone. After a few weeks, Janine got a job working as a salesperson in a big clothing store. She loved her job, and she made many friends at work. Then she joined a health club and met more people. Now Janine is very happy in New York. She says she will never move.

_____ Janie moved to New York after college.

_____ She joined a health club and met more people.

_____ She hated New York because it was so big and she was lonely.

_____ Janie loves New York and wants to stay there.

_____ She got a job and made new friends.

3. Last night's soccer game was the most exciting game I have ever watched. The game was between our team, Greenwell, and Sherborn. Greenwell scored a goal immediately. Then Sherborn got one. Then Greenwell got a second goal, and Sherborn did too. At the half the score was 2 to 2. Neither team got a goal in the second half, so the game went into overtime. Finally, Greenwell's star player kicked a goal and we won! What a great game!

_____ Greenwell and Sherborn each scored two goals in the first half.

_____ Greenwell won the game in overtime.

_____ Greenwell scored the first goal.

_____ The two teams were tied at the half.

Be an Active Reader

BEFORE YOU READ

A. Discuss these questions with a partner.

1. Do you like to tell stories? What kind of stories do you like to tell?

2. Why do you think people create and tell stories?

3. Did anything ever happen to you that seemed like bad luck, but then turned out to be good luck? Or, did anything ever happen to you that seemed like good luck, but then turned out to be bad luck?

4. Talk to some older people, such as your parents or grandparents, and find out what kinds of stories they like to tell. Share their ideas with your classmates.

Preview the Vocabulary

The words in the box are boldfaced in the story. Work with a partner and do the exercise that follows.

```
┌─────────────────────────────────────────────────┐
│                 Words to Watch                  │
│                                                 │
│   neighbors        congratulated    blamed      │
│   valuable         misfortune       complain    │
│   accident         terrible                     │
│   comforted        suddenly                      │
└─────────────────────────────────────────────────┘
```

B. Read the following sentences. Then match the boldfaced words and phrases with the definitions below. Write the correct letter in the space provided. If you need more help, read the sentence in the story where the word appears and think about how it is used.

_____ 1. We have new **neighbors**. They just bought the house next door to ours.

_____ 2. My friend **comforted** me when I broke my arm.

_____ 3. We saw a **terrible** movie last night. I hated it.

_____ 4. This painting is a **valuable** piece of art, so be very careful with it.

_____ 5. Everyone **congratulated** me when I won the contest.

_____ 6. We were playing tennis when **suddenly** it started to rain.

_____ 7. He was in a car **accident** on his way to work. Luckily no one was hurt.

_____ 8. We had the **misfortune** of being in the airport when the storm hit.

_____ 9. She **blamed** her cat for breaking the vase.

_____ 10. The students **complain** when their teacher gives too much homework.

    a. to say or think that someone is responsible for something bad

    b. to tell someone that you are happy because something good happened to someone

    c. to say that you are not satisfied or are unhappy about something

    d. worth a lot of money

    e. quickly and unexpectedly

    f. something that happens because of bad luck

    g. to make someone feel better by being kind to him or her

    h. someone who lives very near you

    i. very bad

    j. a situation in which someone is hurt or something is damaged

Read with a Purpose

You are going to read an old Chinese story. The story is about an old man whose horse ran away. This caused many other things to happen. Take a few minutes to preview the story. Read the title of the story. Look at the pictures. Read the story to find out why the story is called "Things Happen for a Reason."

As you read the story, number the sentences on the opposite page so they tell the story in the correct order.

Things Happen for a Reason

1   People often say, "Things happen for a reason." There is an old Chinese story that parents often tell their children. The story is about a man named Cai who lived long ago. Cai lived in a small village with his only son. He didn't have much money, but he owned a fine horse. One day, when Cai went to feed the horse, he discovered that it had run away. He looked all over his village, but he couldn't find the  horse. He asked everyone about the horse, but no one had seen it. Now Cai didn't have a horse. When his **neighbors** heard the news, they came over to **comfort** him. "Poor Cai," they said. "How **terrible** to lose a **valuable** horse." But Cai just smiled and said, "Who knows what is good luck or bad luck?"

2   The next day, Cai's horse came home during the night, but it did not return alone. Another horse was standing next to Cai's horse. It was a beautiful white horse. Now Cai had two horses. When the neighbors heard this news, they came over to

Cai's house again. This time they wanted to **congratulate** Cai on his good luck. "How lucky you are," they said. "Such a beautiful horse has **suddenly** appeared out of nowhere." Cai smiled again and said, "Who knows if this is good luck or not?"

3   A few days later, Cai's only son had an **accident**. He was riding the new white horse.

When the horse jumped over a large rock, young Cai fell off. The horse was fine, but young Cai broke his leg. The villagers thought this was a terrible **misfortune**. Again they came to Cai's house to comfort him. They **blamed** the white horse for bringing bad luck to Cai's family. Old Cai, however, did not **complain**. "Wait and see" was all that he would say.

4   A week later, a group of soldiers[1] came to the village. They found all the young men and took them to fight in a war. Young Cai was still in bed with a broken leg, so he did not have to go into the army. Most of the young men in the village died in the fighting, but young Cai was saved.

Finally, the villagers understood the wisdom[2] of old Cai. Sometimes what looks like bad luck may not be so bad. Sometimes misfortune may be a blessing in disguise.[3]

[2]***wisdom:*** *knowledge gained from experience over a long period of time*

[3]***blessing in disguise:*** *something that seems to be bad but that you later realize is good*

____ Soldiers came to the village to take all young men to fight in a war.

____ Cai's son fell off the beautiful white horse and broke his leg.

____ Cai's horse ran away.

____ Cai's horse returned with a beautiful white horse.

____ Young Cai did not have to go into the army because he was in bed with a broken leg.

____ Many young men died in the fighting, but young Cai was saved.

AFTER YOU READ

After you have read "Things Happen for a Reason," complete the exercises below.

Check Your Comprehension

A. True or False? Write T (True) or F (False) next to each statement. If a statement is false, rewrite it to make it true.

> **Example**
>
> _F_ Cai had a lot of money. _(Cai didn't have a lot of money.)_

_____ 1. Cai had a fine horse that ran away. _____

_____ 2. Young Cai broke his leg. _____

_____ 3. Young Cai had to fight in the army. _____

_____ 4. Cai's horse returned with an old gray horse. _____

_____ 5. The people in the village finally understood the wisdom of Cai.

_____

Test Your Vocabulary

B. Choose the word or phrase that best completes each sentence. Circle the letter.

1. He was riding his new motorcycle when he had a(n)_____.
   a. accident
   b. neighbor
   c. congratulated

2. Alice _____ that she had too much work to do.
   a. complained
   b. comforted
   c. congratulated

3. Many buildings were destroyed in the _____ storm.
   a. misfortune
   b. terrible
   c. comfort

4. I want to _____ you on your fine work.
   a. congratulate
   b. suddenly
   c. comfort

5. Our new _____ moved here from Greece.
   a. accident
   b. terrible
   c. neighbors

6. We were surprised when the little boy _____ started crying.
   a. suddenly
   b. terrible
   c. blame

7. Her jewelry is very _____.
   a. neighbor
   b. valuable
   c. accident

8. I had the _____ of being in the elevator when it broke.
   a. misfortune
   b. suddenly
   c. terrible

9. Don't _____ Mary for making this mess. She wasn't here today.
   a. blame
   b. comfort
   c. congratulate

10. Please try to _____ the baby. She's crying.
    a. blame
    b. comfort
    c. congratulate

Sharpen Your Vocabulary Skills

USING CONTEXT CLUES

One way to understand the meaning of a new word is to look it up in a dictionary. But you do not always have to take the time to use a dictionary. Sometimes you can guess the meaning of a new word. One way to guess the meaning of a new word is to use the context—the words and sentences around the word.

TIP The context of a word can give you a lot of information about the word. It can tell you the word's part of speech. It can also give you information about the meaning of the word.

Do you know what *village* means? If not, you can use the context of the word to guess what it means. From the sentence you know that a village is a place where Cai lives. You also know that it is small. From that information, you can guess that a village is like a town.

A. Read each of the sentences below. Try to guess the meaning of the underlined words. Do not use a dictionary.

1. The bus leaves in ten minutes at 9:30. It's already 9:20. I'll have to <u>rush</u> to catch it.

   _____

2. Alvin always <u>brags</u> about how smart he is. Yesterday he told me that he's the smartest person in the whole school.

   _____

3. My grandfather is growing <u>deaf</u>. He can't hear what I'm saying unless I talk very loudly.

   _____

4. It <u>seldom</u> snows in my hometown. In the past ten years it has only snowed one time.

   _____

5. She told us a <u>humorous</u> story about her first dinner with her new mother-in-law. It was such a funny story that we couldn't stop laughing.

   _____

6. The next day, Cai's horse came home during the night, but it did not <u>return</u> alone.

   _____

7. He didn't have much money, but he <u>owned</u> a fine horse.

_____

8. One day, when he went to feed the horse, he discovered that it had <u>run away</u>. He looked all over his village, but he couldn't find the horse.

_____

WORK WITH WORDS

Irregular Verbs

Most verbs in English are regular. Regular verbs add _-ed_ to make the past tense. English also has many irregular verbs. You need to recognize the past-tense forms of irregular verbs when you read.

You can use a dictionary to find the past-tense forms of irregular verbs. Look at the entry below for the word _come_. The second form (_came_) is the past tense.

come /kʌm/ _v_ **came, come, coming** [1]

A. Look at the list of irregular verbs from the article. Write the past tense of each verb.

1. take _____

2. come _____

3. fall _____

4. break _____

5. think _____

6. find _____

7. understand _____

B. Write a sentence in the past tense for each of the words on the list.

1. take _____

2. come _____

3. fall _____

4. break _____

5. think _____

6. find _____

7. understand _____

Word Families

C. Complete the following sentences with the correct word from the chart. Be sure to use the correct form of the word.

Noun	Verb	Adjective
discovery	discover	
preference	prefer	preferable
congratulations	congratulate	congratulatory
beauty	beautify	beautiful
value	value	valuable

1. _____ on your engagement!

2. Do you _____ coffee or tea?

3. I was so impressed with the _____ of the Grand Canyon that I took a whole roll of pictures.

4. He has a very _____ coin collection.

5. I finally _____ who sent me the flowers.

6. My friends _____ me on the birth of my daughter.

7. She is wearing a _____ new dress.

8. The scientist made an important scientific _____ about the moon.

Pronoun Reference

D. Read the following sentences. Notice each underlined pronoun and look for the noun that it refers to.

1. There is an old Chinese story about a man named Cai who lived long ago with <u>his</u> only son. <u>He</u> didn't have much money, but he owned a fine horse. One day, when <u>he</u> went to feed the horse, he discovered that <u>it</u> had run away.

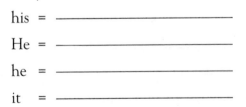

his = —————————————

He = —————————————

he = —————————————

it = —————————————

2. The next day, Cai's horse returned home during the night, but <u>it</u> did not return alone.

it = _____

3. Another horse was standing next to Cai's horse. <u>It</u> was a beautiful white horse.

It = _____

4. Again the neighbors came over. This time <u>they</u> wanted to congratulate Cai on <u>his</u> good luck. "How lucky you are," they said.

they = _____

his = _____

5. A few days later, Cai's only son had an accident. <u>He</u> was riding the new white horse when the horse jumped over a large rock. Young Cai fell off the horse and broke <u>his</u> leg.

He = _____

his = _____

6. A week later, soldiers came to the village. <u>They</u> found all the young men and took <u>them</u> to fight in a war.

They = _____

them = _____

Synonyms and Antonyms

E. Write an S if the words are synonyms. Write an A if the words are antonyms. Use your dictionary to look up the meanings of unfamiliar words.

1. fortune   misfortune   _____

2. suddenly   gradually   _____

3. terrible   awful   _____

4. valuable   worthless   _____

Sum It Up

Reread "Things Happen for a Reason." Make a list of the main events in the story. Then, in your own words, tell a partner what the story was about.

_____

_____

_____

_____

_____

_____

_____

_____

Express Your Ideas

A. Discuss these questions in small groups.

1. Do you agree with the expression "Things happen for a reason"? Why or why not?

2. What is the luckiest thing that ever happened to you? When did it happen?

3. Do you think telling stories is a good way to teach lessons? Why or why not?

4. Many cultures have proverbs about luck and fortune. Can you think of expressions in your first language about luck?

5. Read and discuss these proverbs about luck from various cultures:

   "Luck favors those who prepare for it." (Chinese proverb)

   "Better an ounce of luck than a pound of gold." (Yiddish proverb)

   "Throw a lucky man in the sea, and he will come up with a fish in his mouth." (Arab proverb)

   "Luck sometimes visits a fool, but it never sits down with him." (German proverb)

   "Go and wake up your luck." (Persian proverb)

B. Choose one of the questions from page 82 and write a paragraph about it.

_____

_____

_____

_____

_____

_____

_____

_____

_____

_____

Explore the Web

Do some research on the Web about a story, fairytale, or folktale from your home country. Make a list of the events in the story or draw several pictures that show the sequence of events in the story. Tell the story to your classmates or act it out with several of your classmates.

Read Faster

Each row begins with a two-word expression. Circle the expressions in each row that are the same as the first expression. Don't worry if you see an expression you don't know. Just work as fast as you can. Try to complete the exercise in thirty seconds. When you have finished, check your answers on page 156. Figure out how many answers you got right and complete the chart on page 159. This will help you see your progress.

1.	well-made	well-said	well-made	poorly made	well-made
2.	look up	look up	look over	look at	look up
3.	work out	walk out	work out	work out	work on
4.	make up	make up	made up	make out	make up
5.	get in	get in	get it	got in	get in
6.	rain hat	brain hat	rain hat	rain hard	rain hat
7.	summer school	summer school	summer vacation	summer school	ski school
8.	candy bar	candy bar	candy cane	candy bag	candy bar
9.	flat tire	flat time	flat tire	free tire	flat tire
10.	tall tale	telltale	tall tale	tall tale	tall tile

Have Some Fun

Work with a group of three or four students. Make up a story that teaches a lesson. Follow these steps.

1. Think of a lesson for the story and write it on the line.

   _____

2. Make a list of the characters in the story.

   _____

   _____

   _____

   _____

3. Choose a time and place for your story.

_____

4. Write a title.

_____

5. Make a list of events in the story. Be sure to put the events in the correct time order.

_____

_____

_____

_____

_____

_____

6. Draw some pictures to go with the story.

7. Choose someone from your group to tell the story to the class.

CHAPTER 5

Read Quickly
Scanning for Information

Old Boston

New Boston

Look quickly at the two photographs of Boston. Discuss what you see with a partner. Try to find details in the pictures that show the differences between Boston in the past and Boston now.

Make a list of the differences you see between the two photos.

_____

_____

_____

_____

_____

_____

> When you looked quickly at each of the photos to locate certain details, you scanned it. Scanning is a skill that you can use to become a better reader.

Sharpen Your Reading Skills

SCANNING

Good readers read at different speeds for different purposes. For example, you might read slowly and carefully when you are reading a textbook. However, when you are only looking for a specific piece of information, you might read quickly. This is called scanning. Scanning is an important reading skill that requires fast reading.

Scanning is a way to read quickly in order to find specific information. When you scan, you move your eyes quickly across the text. You do not stop to read every word. To scan you need to:

1. Know the specific information you are looking for: a name, a date, a time, a keyword.
2. Ignore the words and information that aren't important for your purpose.
3. Move your eyes quickly across the text until you find the information, and then stop reading.

Scanning a Newspaper Index

A. A newspaper is divided into sections. The sections are often labeled A, B, C, D, and so on. Most newspapers have an index on the first page. The index tells you the topic and page number of each section. Scan the index to answer the questions below.

Arts and Entertainment	B2
Business	C1
Help Wanted	C5
Local News	B1
National News	A1
Opinion	A10
Science & Technology	C5
Sports	D1
Television	B5
Weather	B9
World News	A3

Example

If you want to read about the news around the world, where would you look? In Section A, on page 3.

1. If you want to see if it is going to rain tonight, where would you look?
   _____

2. Where would you look to find the final score of yesterday's soccer game?
   _____

3. Where would you look to see what television shows are on tonight?
   _____

4. If you were trying to find a part-time job, what section would you check?
   _____

5. Where would you look to read about news in your city? _____

Scanning a Menu

B. Scan the menu to answer the questions below.

∾PINE STREET RESTAURANT ∾

251 Pine Street   Open 11 A.M.–10 P.M. daily

Soups		Salads	
Clam Chowder cup $4.50 bowl $6.95		Garden Salad	$2.50
Chicken		Caesar Salad	
and Rice cup $3.50 bowl $5.95		with Grilled Chicken	$7.00
Vegetable Rice cup $3.50 bowl $5.95		Spinach Salad	$6.00

∾ Sandwiches ∾
All sandwiches come with French fries and coleslaw

Cold Sandwiches		Hot Sandwiches	
Tuna fish	$4.50	Roast Beef	$7.50
Bacon, Lettuce, and Tomato	$4.95	Grilled Chicken	$7.00
Seafood Salad	$4.95	Hamburger	$5.75
Veggie and Cheese	$4.85	Meatball Sandwich	$6.00
Turkey Club	$4.75	Steak Sandwich	$6.00
		Grilled Cheese and Tomato	$3.50

Desserts		Beverages	
Cheesecake	$3.95	Soda	$1.75
Fruit Pie	$3.95	Coffee/Tea	$1.50
Chocolate Cake	$3.95	Juice	$1.50
Ice Cream	$3.00		

Example

What is the most expensive soup on the menu?
A bowl of clam chowder

---

1. What do the sandwiches come with? _____

2. How many types of salads does the Pine Street Restaurant offer?
_____

3. What is the least expensive sandwich on the menu? _____

4. What time does the Pine Street Restaurant open? _____

5. How much would a garden salad and a steak sandwich cost?
_____

Scanning a TV Guide

C. Scan the TV guide to answer the questions below.

Channel	8:00	8:30	9:00	9:30	10:00
TV Tonight					
2	The Game Show	Friends	Inside Hollywood	Tours and Travels	Local Weather
4	Soccer: Brazil versus Italy (8:00–10:30)				
5	Business Week	Politics Today	Talk about Money	Cops and Robbers	
7	M*A*S*H	I Love Lucy	Seinfeld	Frasier	Sports News
10	News Hour		Women's College Volleyball		Late Show
12	Arts & Antiques	Decorating with Diana		Highlights of History	
24	Learn Spanish at Home	Cooking Made Easy	You and Your Health	The Fix-It Man	Gardening Tips
37	Movie: The Lord of the Rings: The Fellowship of the Ring				

Example

Who is Brazil playing in tonight's soccer game on channel 4? <u>Italy</u>

---

1. What channel is M*A*S*H on? _____

2. Which channel has a show about history? _____

3. Which show will give you decorating ideas? _____

4. What time can you watch a show about antiques? _____

5. What show is on channel 5 at 9:30? _____

6. What time can you find out about your local weather? _____

7. What time can you tune in to learn Spanish? _____

8. What channel should you watch to see who won tonight's basketball game? _____

9. What movie can you watch on channel 37 tonight? _____

Scanning the Classified Ads

D. Scan the classified ads to answer the questions below.

Arlington Street, 2 bedroom, kitchen, living room, dining room, walk to subway. $1200. 555-5555

Avon Street, 1 bedroom apt., 2nd floor of Victorian house, owner lives downstairs, all utilities included. $1400. Call 555-5555

Bridgeton Street, modern 1 bedroom apt., newly painted. Available January 1. $1550. Call 555-5555

Franklin Street, new to market! Beautiful 3 bedroom house with eat-in kitchen, large family room, new furnace and hot water heater. $3000. Call 555-5555

Gloucester Street, 1 bedroom apt., Large kitchen, walk to subway, new carpet, no pets, no smoking. $850. Call 555-5555

Hammond Street, 1 bedroom apt., hardwood floors, 3rd floor walk-up, river view, air-conditioning. $1800. Call 555-5555

Jensen Street, sunny 1 bedroom apt. with fireplace, cats but no dogs. Close to downtown but quiet area. $950. Call 555-5555

Lowell Street, 3 bedroom apt., total 6 rooms, clean, first floor of two family house, laundry, yard. $1300. Call 555-5555

Staniford Street, spacious 2 bedroom apt., 1 minute walk to bus stop. Storage area and 1 car parking included. $1000. Call 555-5555

Water Street, Brick, 6 room house, 2 bedrooms, garden, 2 car garage, air-conditioning. Call 555-5555 for rental fees

---

Example

How much is the apartment on Hammond Street? $1800 a month

---

1. Which apartment would not interest you if you have a cat? _____

2. How many rooms does the house on Lowell Street have? _____

3. Which apartments are close to a bus stop or subway? _____

4. When is the Bridgeton Street apartment available? _____

5. How many places have air-conditioning? _____

6. If you like to garden, which place would interest you? _____

Be an Active Reader

A. Discuss these questions with a partner.

1. Do you like to dance?

2. Did you ever take dance lessons?

3. What is your favorite kind of dance?

4. What dances are popular in your culture?

5. Are there any holidays in your country where people do special dances?

6. Does your culture have any traditional dances?

Preview the Vocabulary

The words in the box are boldfaced in the article. Work with a partner and do the exercise that follows.

> **Words to Watch**
>
> | | | |
> |---|---|---|
> | back and forth | festival | simple |
> | gradually | combination | huge |
> | approve | traditional | |
> | brave | celebrated | |

B. Read the following sentences. Then match the boldfaced words and phrases with the definitions on the opposite page. Write the correct letter in the space provided. If you need more help, read the sentence in the article where the word appears and think about how it is used.

_____ 1. She keeps walking **back and forth** in front of the door.

_____ 2. He was **brave** enough to go back into the burning house to save his dog.

_____ 3. I miss the **traditional** food and music of my home country.

_____ 4. You can do this math problem. It's very **simple**.

_____ 5. It took a long time, but **gradually** I lost 20 pounds.

_____ 6. People dance in the streets during the spring **festival**.

_____ 7. We **celebrated** Ian's birthday at a restaurant.

_____ 8. They live in a **huge** house. It has eight bedrooms.

_____ 9. I do not **approve** of drinking and driving.

_____10. The **combination** of furniture in their living room—some old and some new—makes it very unusual.

a. to do something special because of a special occasion
b. to believe that someone or something is good or acceptable
c. in a way that happens slowly over time
d. not difficult or complicated
e. dealing with danger, pain, or difficult situations with courage
f. two or more things that are put together
g. in one direction and then in the opposite direction
h. a series of special events, such as musical performances, that take place over several days
i. relating to the way of doing something that has existed for a long time
j. very big

Read with a Purpose

You are going to read an article that discusses many aspects of dance. For example, you will read about the history of dance and why people dance. Before you read the article, complete the first two columns of the chart.

What I know about dance	What I want to know about dance	What I learned about dance

As you read the article, look for examples to support main ideas. The phrases *for example* and *for instance* often introduce examples. Complete the chart on pages 95–96.

Let's Dance

Why People Dance

1   Most people like to dance. This may be because moving the body in rhythm[1] is a natural way to show our feelings. Look at children. Children often jump up and down when they are excited about something. Sometimes they move **back and forth** quietly when they are relaxed. Dancing is also lots of fun. Many people dance just to enjoy themselves.

An Ancient Art

2   Dance is almost as old as human civilization. Cave paintings[2] in Africa and Southern Europe show pictures of people dancing. These pictures were painted hundreds of thousands of years ago. Dance later became part of religion. People danced for many reasons. For example, they danced to bring rain, to make crops grow, and to bring good hunting. Warriors[3] performed dances too. They danced to feel **brave** before a battle.

Let's Dance

3   Every culture has its own **traditional** dances. They often began as **simple** dances of ordinary people. **Gradually**, people added specific moves and steps. Some dances became very formal with rules for the dancers. The first formal social dances were held in Japan 1,500 years ago.

Dancing to Celebrate

4   Dancing plays a major part in many holidays and **festivals** around the world. For example, in the spring, the people of Central and South America **celebrate** a holiday called Carnaval. For five days, people of all ages dance in the streets wearing beautiful costumes. They dance to a kind of music called samba. Another example of dancing at holidays takes place in China. People there celebrate the Chinese New Year with a traditional dance called the Dragon Dance. The Dragon Dance is performed by a group of dancers. The dancers carry a huge dragon

[1] **rhythm:** *a regular repeated pattern of sounds in music or speech.*

[2] **cave painting:** *a picture painted on the wall of a cave*

[3] **warrior:** *a soldier, especially an experienced and skillful one*

made of silk, paper, and bamboo through the streets of the city. In India, traditional dances are also performed at festivals throughout the year. The dances have close links with the Hindu religion. The dances tell stories about the Hindu gods.

Changing Styles

5   Many new dances have appeared over the last 200 years. For instance, in the 1800s, a new dance called the waltz became popular in Europe and North America. The waltz is a type of ballroom dance with gliding turns. Some people did not **approve** of the waltz because men and women danced too close to each other. Another type of dancing that became popular in the 1800s was tap dancing. Tap dancing is a **combination** of African, Irish, and English dances that developed among African Americans. In the 1950s, rock 'n' roll became popular. It gave birth to disco, which was danced all over the world in the 1970s.

Carnaval is a special time for people in Central and South America to dance in the streets.

The Dragon Dance is an important part of the Chinese New Year celebrations.

Indian dancers wear beautiful costumes. Their dances tell stories.

Main Idea: People danced for many reasons.
Examples:
1. They danced to bring rain.
2. _____
3. _____
4. _____

(Continued on next page.)

Main Idea: Dancing plays a major part in many holidays and festivals.

Examples:

1. _____

2. _____

3. _____

Main Idea: Many new dances have appeared over the last 200 years.

Examples:

1. _____

2. _____

3. _____

4. _____

AFTER YOU READ

Complete the third column in the chart on page 93. Did the article answer any of your questions from the second column? Which ones? Look at the things you wrote in the first column. Were any of your ideas confirmed or rejected in the article? Which ones?

Check Your Comprehension

A. Choose the word or phrase that best completes each sentence. Circle the letter.

1. Children often move back and forth quietly when they are

   _____.

   a. hungry
   b. excited
   c. relaxed

2. The first formal social dances were held in _____ 1,500 years ago.

   a. Japan
   b. Europe
   c. North America

3. Many years ago, people danced to _____.

   a. bring rain and make crops grow
   b. bring good hunting
   c. both "a." and "b."

4. The _____ is a type of ballroom dance with gliding turns.
   a. waltz
   b. samba
   c. tap

5. Rock 'n' roll became popular in the _____.
   a. 1800s
   b. 1980s and 90s
   c. 1950s

Test Your Vocabulary

B. Choose the word or phrase that best completes each sentence and write it in the space below.

back and forth	brave	traditional	simple	gradually
festival	celebrate	huge	approve	combination

1. This is a very _____ dance. Just follow my steps.

2. I love to listen to _____ Irish music.

3. Vitamin C should be taken in _____ with other vitamins.

4. _____, she is beginning to feel better after her illness.

5. She was scared but tried to be _____ during the earthquake.

6. My dog is wagging his tail _____. That means he's happy.

7. The president of the company lives alone in a _____ house.

8. An important film _____ is held every year in Cannes, France.

9. How do you want to _____ New Year's Eve this year?

10. I don't _____ of my daughter staying out late at night.

C. Use a dictionary to determine the part of speech of the underlined word in each of the following sentences. Then write the correct definition.

1. For example, they danced to bring rain, to make <u>crops</u> grow, and to bring good hunting.

   Part of speech: _____

   Definition: _____

2. Gradually, people added specific moves and <u>steps</u>.

Part of speech: _____

Definition: _____

3. For example, in the <u>spring</u> the people of Central and South America celebrate a holiday called Carnaval in which many people dance in the streets wearing beautiful costumes.

Part of speech: _____

Definition: _____

4. They dance to a <u>kind</u> of music called samba.

Part of speech: _____

Definition: _____

Sharpen Your Vocabulary Skills

USING WORD MAPS

When you are learning a new language you need to learn many new words. It can be difficult to remember the meanings of all the new words. One way to help you remember a new word is to make a word map. A word map is a chart that helps you understand and remember the meaning of a word.

Follow these steps. Write the new word in the middle of the map. Then, complete the rest of the map with a definition, a synonym, an antonym, and a picture of the word or a sentence that uses the word. Look at this example of a word map.

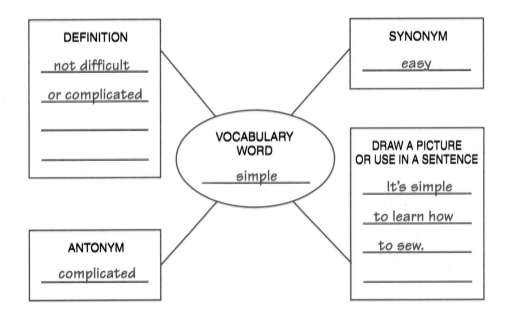

Choose three new words from the article "Let's Dance" that you want to learn and remember. Make a word map for each word.

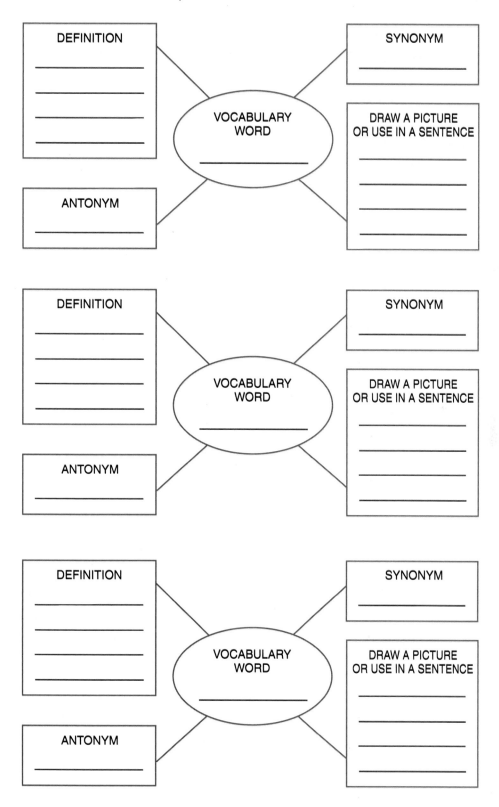

Share your word maps with a partner. Use them to teach your partner the meaning of the words.

WORK WITH WORDS

Commonly Confused Words

Some English words are often confused because their pronunciation or spelling is the same or similar. Study the words in the box and then do the exercise that follows.

it's – it is: <u>*It's*</u> *raining.* **its** – shows possession: *The tree has lost <u>its</u> leaves.* [its = the tree's leaves/the leaves of the tree]
two – 2: *I have <u>two</u> brothers.* **too** – also, more than enough: *José is from Mexico and María is, <u>too</u>.* **to** – a preposition: *I am going <u>to</u> the library to study.*
there – in/at a place: *My dog sleeps over <u>there</u> in the corner.* **they're** – contraction of *they are*: <u>*They're*</u> *late for class again.* **their** – shows possession: *Mr. and Mrs. Lee love <u>their</u> new house.* [their = Mr. and Mrs. Lee's house]
hear – to perceive sounds with the ear: *Please turn up the TV. I can't <u>hear</u> it.* **here** – in this place: *The book you want is right <u>here</u>.*
loose – not attached firmly, not tight-fitting: *Her pants are <u>loose</u>.* **lose** – to misplace, to be defeated: *I hope our team doesn't <u>lose</u> the basketball game.*
quiet – without noise: *The house was <u>quiet</u> because everyone was asleep.* **quite** – very: *The weather is <u>quite</u> cold here in the winter.*
weak – not strong: *She felt very <u>weak</u> after her long illness.* **week** – the seven-day period from Sunday to Saturday: *There are 52 <u>weeks</u> in a year.*
weather – condition of the air or atmosphere: *The <u>weather</u> here is nice in the summer.* **whether** – shows choice; if: *Tell me <u>whether</u> or not you want to go home.*
whose – possessive form of who: *<u>Whose</u> car this is?* [Who owns this car?] **who's** – who is: <u>*Who's*</u> *riding in my car with me?*

A. Complete the sentences. Choose the correct form of the words in parentheses.

1. Many years ago, some people danced to make (their/there) crops grow.

2. The costumes worn at Carnaval were (quiet/quite) beautiful.

3. (It's/its) not unusual for children to take dance lessons.

4. Some people join dance groups and meet to dance every (weak/week).

5. The traditional dances of some countries tell a story. Audiences don't (hear/here) the story—they see it.

6. The waltz became popular in the 1800s and tap dancing did (to/too/two).

7. In some dances, (it's/its) hard to tell (who's/whose) leading and (who's/whose) following.

8. It is important to wear (loose/lose) clothes if you want to rock 'n' roll.

9. Scientists study the dances of various cultures because the kinds of dances people do can tell a lot about (there/their/they're) way of life.

10. The (weather/whether) in Central and South America is usually warm during Carnaval.

Using Context Clues

B. Read each of the sentences below. Try to guess the meaning of the underlined words. Do not use a dictionary.

1. Dancing is also lots of fun. Many people dance just to <u>enjoy</u> themselves.

   _____

2. Warriors performed dances too. They danced to feel brave before a <u>battle</u>.

   _____

3. For example, in the spring the people of Central and South America celebrate a holiday called Carnaval in which many people dance in the streets wearing beautiful <u>costumes</u>.

   _____

4. They dance to a kind of music called <u>samba</u>.

   _____

5. The <u>waltz</u> is a type of ballroom dance with gliding turns.

   _____

Synonyms and Antonyms

C. Write an S if the words are synonyms. Write an A if the words are antonyms. Use your dictionary to look up the meanings of unfamiliar words.

1. brave   courageous   _____

2. approve   disapprove   _____

3. huge   enormous   _____

4. simple   complicated   _____

5. gradually   slowly   _____

Pronoun Reference

D. Read the following sentences. Notice each underlined pronoun and look for the noun that it refers to.

1. Children often jump up and down when <u>they</u> are excited about something. Sometimes <u>they</u> move back and forth quietly when <u>they</u> are relaxed.

   they = _____

   they = _____

   they = _____

2. People danced for many reasons. For example, <u>they</u> danced to bring rain, to make crops grow, and to bring good hunting.

   they = _____

3. Warriors performed dances too. <u>They</u> danced to feel brave before a battle.

   They = _____

4. Every country has its own traditional dances. <u>They</u> often began as simple dances of ordinary people.

   They = _____

5. In the 1950s, rock 'n' roll became popular. <u>It</u> gave birth to disco, which was danced all over the world.

   It = _____

Sum It Up

Reread "Let's Dance." Make a list of the main points in the article. Then, in your own words, tell a partner what the article was about.

1. _____
2. _____
3. _____
4. _____
5. _____
6. _____

Express Your Ideas

A. Discuss these questions in small groups.

1. There are two main kinds of dancing—theatrical and social. Theatrical dancing is done for the entertainment of other people. Examples include ballet, tap dancing, modern dance, ice dancing, and roller dancing. Do you enjoy watching any of these kinds of dancing? Which ones? Why?

2. Social dancing is when people dance for their own pleasure. Do you think it's fun to dance? What kind of dancing do you like to do?

3. The article says that dance can be used to express emotion. What kinds of dancing do you think express joy? Bravery? What other emotions do dances express?

4. What is your favorite kind of dancing?

B. Choose one of the questions above and write a paragraph about it.

_____

_____

_____

_____

_____

Explore the Web

For thousands of years people have used dance to express the spirit and personality of their culture. Match the dances below with their countries of origin. Use the Internet to help you.

1. ____ Polka
2. ____ Cake Walk
3. ____ Rumba
4. ____ Twist
5. ____ Samba
6. ____ Merengue
7. ____ Jig
8. ____ Tango
9. ____ Waltz
10. ____ Macarena

a. Traditional folk dance of Ireland
b. A dance that started in Spain in 1993
c. Originated in Czechoslovakia around 1835
d. National dance of the Dominican Republic and Haiti
e. Originated in the 1840s in the United States among slaves
f. Cuban and Latin American dance that started in the sixteenth century
g. A Brazilian dance
h. A slow dance that originated in Austria
i. Originated by Chubby Checker in the United States in the 1960s
j. A slow dance from Argentina

Read Faster

Each row begins with a two-word expression. Circle the expressions in each row that are the same as the first expression. Don't worry if you see an expression you don't know. Just work as fast as you can. Try to complete the exercise in thirty seconds. When you have finished, check your answers on page 157. Figure out how many answers you got right and compete the chart on page 159. This will help you see your progress.

1. put on   put out   put over   put on   put in
2. tree top   tee top   top tee   top tree   tree top
3. take out   take out   take on   take over   take it
4. sweet treat   sweat treat   sweet treat   sweet tree   sweat tree
5. get up   get on   get over   get up   get it
6. get along   get alone   get it   get along   get up

7.	flower power	flowing power	power flower	flower tower	flower power
8.	fill out	fill in	fill out	felt it	fill it
9.	tip off	tip top	tip toe	tip off	tip over
10.	topsy turvy	topsy turkey	turvy topsy	topsy turny	topsy turvy

Have Some Fun

Look at the picture for ten seconds. Your teacher will time you. Then cover the picture with your hand and try to answer the questions.

1. How many people are in the drawing? _____

2. How many people are dancing? _____

3. How many are men? _____

4. How many are women? _____

5. Are the women wearing long dresses or short? _____

6. Are the men wearing bow ties or traditional neckties? _____

7. What time is it? _____

8. What is the reason for this party? _____

9. Are there any balloons in the picture? _____

10. Is anyone eating? _____

CHAPTER 6

Evaluate Information
Distinguishing Facts from Opinions

Look at the photograph of the Walt Disney Concert Hall in Los Angeles. Make a list of the things you see. Discuss your list with a partner.

_____   _____

_____   _____

Which statements are facts that can be checked and proven to be true?
Which statements are opinions that tell someone's ideas about the new Walt Disney Concert Hall?

Fact	Opinion	1. The Walt Disney Concert Hall was completed in October 2003.
Fact	Opinion	2. Architect Frank Gehry designed the Walt Disney Concert Hall.
Fact	Opinion	3. Gehry created a wonderful design for the concert hall.
Fact	Opinion	4. The Walt Disney Concert Hall is a beautiful piece of modern architecture that is worth visiting.
Fact	Opinion	5. The Disney Concert Hall is 293,000 square feet in size and has 2,265 seats.
Fact	Opinion	6. It is certainly one of the best concert halls in the world.
Fact	Opinion	7. It cost $274 million to build the Disney Concert Hall.
Fact	Opinion	8. The people of Los Angeles are happy about the concert hall.

When you looked at the photo and read the statements about the Walt Disney Concert Hall, you decided which information was fact and which was opinion. Learning to understand the difference between facts and opinions is a valuable skill.

Sharpen Your Reading Skills

DISTINGUISHING FACTS FROM OPINIONS

Whenever you read, it is important for you to think about whether you are reading something that is a fact or an opinion. Think about this statement:

New York is the most exciting city in the United States.

Do you agree or disagree with the statement? You can agree or disagree with the statement because it is an opinion. You cannot prove whether New York is the most exciting city or not. Opinions are beliefs that you cannot prove.

Now think about this statement:

New York City is 204 miles (328 km) from Washington, DC.

You cannot agree or disagree with this statement because it is a fact. You can prove that it is true by measuring the distance. Facts can be checked. They can be observed, counted, measured, and recorded. Facts are different from opinions because they can be proven to be true.

> A **fact** is a statement that you can prove to be true. An **opinion** is a statement that describes someone's feelings or beliefs about a topic. Learning to decide if a statement is a fact or an opinion will help you understand more about what you read.

Sometimes writers use certain words that show opinions. Here are some words that can indicate opinions.

bad	believe	best	feel
good	greatest	most important	least
may	might	probably	
should	should not	worst	

A. Read each statement and decide if it is a fact or an opinion. Write F (Fact) or O (Opinion) on the line.

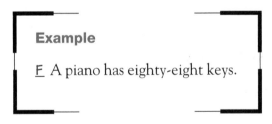

Example

F A piano has eighty-eight keys.

_____ 1. Peru is the third-largest country in South America.
_____ 2. Tea is the best drink.
_____ 3. Johann Sebastian Bach was the greatest composer of all time.
_____ 4. Jupiter has twenty-eight moons.
_____ 5. Johann Sebastian Bach was born in 1685 and died in 1750.
_____ 6. The Pacific Ocean is the deepest of all the world's oceans.
_____ 7. Mark Twain's best book is *The Adventures of Tom Sawyer*.
_____ 8. Tigers live in the forests, mountains, and plains of Asia and Indonesia.
_____ 9. Hamsters make terrible pets.

B. Now read each paragraph and the statements that follow. Circle *Fact* or *Opinion*.

1.   The Rock and Roll Hall of Fame and Museum opened on April 2, 1998, in Cleveland, Ohio. Its purpose is to educate people about the history and importance of rock-and-roll music. The museum collects and exhibits objects from major rock-and-roll artists from the past and the present. The collection includes musical instruments, letters, and handwritten songs. It also has rock stars' clothes and even shoes! If you are interested in rock and roll, you will love this museum.

Fact	Opinion	**a.** The Rock and Roll Hall of Fame and Museum opened on April 2, 1998.
Fact	Opinion	**b.** The museum has musical instruments, letters, and handwritten song lyrics.
Fact	Opinion	**c.** If you are interested in rock and roll, you will love this museum.

2.   The Philadelphia Flower Show is the largest indoor flower show in the world. Over 275,000 people go every year to see the amazing flower arrangements that are created by experts. The show lasts for a week. In addition to seeing the flowers, you can listen to lectures and watch demonstrations. There are lots of beautiful flowers and vases that you can buy at reasonable prices. It is a great event and lots of fun for people of all ages.

Fact	Opinion	**a.** The Philadelphia Flower Show is the largest indoor flower show in the world.
Fact	Opinion	**b.** The show lasts for a week.
Fact	Opinion	**c.** It is a great event and lots of fun for people of all ages.

3.   There are many types of pets, but cats make the best pets. I am not the only one who feels this way. In ancient times cats were loved for their beauty and their ability to hunt. The ancient Egyptians brought cats into their homes as pets. They treated their pet cats like members of the family. Throughout history, people have loved cats because they are curious and independent. There is no better pet than a cat.

Fact	Opinion	**a.** The ancient Egyptians brought cats into their homes as pets.
Fact	Opinion	**b.** There are many types of pets, but cats make the best pets.
Fact	Opinion	**c.** There is no better pet than a cat.

4. Pompeii is one of the most interesting places I have ever been to. It was an old city in Italy that was destroyed when the volcano Mount Vesuvius erupted in A.D. 79. The city disappeared for hundreds of years, but it was never completely forgotten. From around 1500 until now, archaeologists have been uncovering Pompeii. It is wonderful that visitors today can go to Pompeii and see what life was like in A.D. 79.

Fact　　Opinion　　**a.** Pompeii is one of the most interesting places I have ever been to.

Fact　　Opinion　　**b.** Pompeii was destroyed by the eruption of Mount Vesuvius in A.D. 79.

Fact　　Opinion　　**c.** It is wonderful that visitors today can go to Pompeii and see what life was like in A.D. 79.

5. Knitting is a very simple craft that is becoming more and more popular among young people. It is a relaxing and creative hobby that is easy to learn. All you need to knit are two knitting needles and some yarn. Once you learn the basics of knitting, you can do it anytime. It's a great hobby because you can make beautiful hats, scarves, or even sweaters while you are watching television or just talking to friends!

Fact　　Opinion　　**a.** All you need to knit are two knitting needles and some yarn.

Fact　　Opinion　　**b.** Knitting is a relaxing and creative hobby that is easy to learn.

Fact　　Opinion　　**c.** It's a great hobby because you can make beautiful hats, scarves, or even sweaters while you are watching television or just talking to friends!

6. Ieoh Ming Pei was born in 1917 in Canton, China. He came to the United States in 1935 to study architecture at the Massachusetts Institute of Technology and at the Harvard Graduate School of Design. He has designed more than fifty projects in the United States and abroad. Some of his most famous designs include the Pyramid at the Louvre in Paris, France; the John F. Kennedy Library near Boston, Massachusetts; and the Jacob Javits Center in New York City. I. M. Pei is a great architect who creates wonderful designs.

Fact　　Opinion　　**a.** Ieoh Ming Pei was born in 1917 in Canton, China.

Fact　　Opinion　　**b.** He has designed more than fifty projects in the United States and abroad.

Fact　　Opinion　　**c.** I. M. Pei is a great architect who creates wonderful designs.

Be an Active Reader

BEFORE YOU READ

A. Answer the following questions.

1. What sports do you like to play? What sports do you like to watch? Complete the chart below.

	I play (participate in) this sport.	I like to watch this sport.	I don't play or watch this sport.
bowling			
swimming			
golf			
soccer			
baseball			
basketball			
tennis			
roller blading			
skiing			
ice hockey			
other			

2. Find a partner and compare your answers.

3. What is the most popular sport in your class? What is the least popular sport?

4. Who is your favorite athlete? Why?

Preview the Vocabulary

The words in the box are boldfaced in the article. Work with a partner and do the exercise that follows.

> **Words to Watch**
>
> athlete   championship   generations
> outstanding   hit   famous
> nickname   celebrities
> teenagers   fashionable

B. Read the following sentences. Then match the boldfaced words and phrases with the definitions below. Write the correct letter in the space provided. If you need more help, read the sentence in the article where the word appears and think about how it is used.

_____ 1. John is the captain of the basketball team, and he also plays soccer and hockey. He's a great **athlete**.

_____ 2. Do you think **teenagers** are too young to be good drivers?

_____ 3. You can see lots of **celebrities** in Hollywood because it's the center of the movie industry.

_____ 4. Lisa is the star of our show. Her singing and dancing are **outstanding**.

_____ 5. Our team won the basketball **championship** and received a trophy.

_____ 6. My sister loves clothes and wears all the latest styles. She is very **fashionable**.

_____ 7. Daniel's **nickname** is Dan.

_____ 8. Her new song is a big **hit**. All the radio stations are playing it constantly.

_____ 9. Three **generations** of people in my family—my grandmother, my mother, and I—have lived in this house.

_____ 10. Einstein is a **famous** mathematician.

a. excellent

b. a shorter form of someone's real name

c. someone who is good at sports

d. a movie, song, or play that is very successful

e. a famous person

f. someone who is between thirteen and nineteen years old

g. a competition to find the best player or team in a particular sport

h. all the people who are about the same age, especially in a family

i. popular, especially for a short time

j. known about or recognized by a lot of people

Read with a Purpose

You are going to read an article about soccer player David Beckham. Before you read the article, complete the first two columns of the chart.

What I know about Beckham	What I want to know about Beckham	What I learned about Beckham

As you read the article, complete the chart on the opposite page by writing in five more facts and five more opinions.

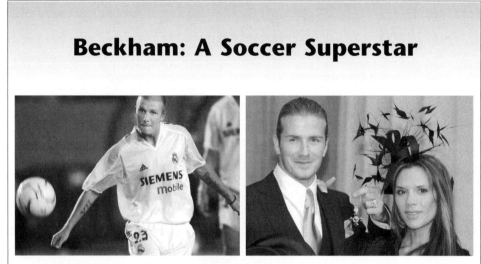

Beckham: A Soccer Superstar

1   Who is the best-known **athlete** in the world? David Beckham should be on any list of famous athletes. He is less well known in the United States because soccer is not as popular in the United States as it is in other countries. Americans even have a different name for soccer. Almost everyone else calls it football. But in most of the world, Beckham is a major **celebrity**. People all over the world have heard of him. He is a soccer superstar and one of the best English soccer players of all time.

A Great Player

2   David Beckham was born in 1975 in England. He grew up in London and joined the team of Manchester United as a **teenager**. Beckham won the Professional Football Association (PFA) Young Player of the Year award in 1997. He has played on England's national team as well as Manchester United. As a midfielder, Beckham helped both teams win many **championships**. His free kicks and skillful passing[1] are **outstanding**. In 2000, Beckham won second place as World Footballer of the Year.

A Fashionable Celebrity

3   Beckham is **famous** not only as a soccer star, but also as a **fashionable** celebrity. Newspaper and television reporters love Beckham. They often talk and write about his clothes and haircuts. He dresses very well, and people like to copy his style. When Beckham gets a new style of haircut, it becomes a major news story.

[1]**passing:** *kicking, throwing, or hitting a ball to another member of your team*

The new style catches on, and soon lots of people are getting haircuts just like Beckham's. In 1999, Beckham married a beautiful singer named Victoria Adams. Victoria was a member of the popular singing group the Spice Girls. Her name in this group was Posh Spice. Beckham also has a **nickname**, Becks. The Beckhams have two sons, Brooklyn and Romeo.

A Beckham in the News

4   One of the biggest sports stories ever was in 2003 when Beckham was traded to the team Real Madrid in Spain. The cost of the trade was 41 million U.S. dollars. Beckham described the move to Real Madrid as "a dream come true." Later that year, Queen Elizabeth gave England's highest honor to Beckham. She appointed Beckham an Officer of the Order of the British Empire (OBE). This same year, the movie *Bend It Like Beckham* became a popular **hit**. It was a wonderful movie about an English girl from an Indian family who dreams of becoming a successful soccer player.

Soccer's Growing Popularity

5   Soccer is becoming more popular in the United States, especially among younger **generations**. More children are playing on soccer teams. As they grow older, they keep on playing soccer. As adults, they watch more soccer matches and continue supporting the sport. Now, there are surely children in the United States who look up to Beckham and dream of becoming the next David Beckham.

Facts	Opinions
David Beckham was born in 1975 in England.	His free kicks and skillful passing are outstanding.
1.	1.
2.	2.
3.	3.
4.	4.
5.	5.

AFTER YOU READ

Fill in the third column in the chart on page 113. Did the article answer any of your questions from the second column? Which ones? Look at the things you wrote in the first column. Were any of your ideas confirmed or rejected in the article? Which ones?

Check Your Comprehension

A. True or False? Write T (True) or F (False) next to each statement. If a statement is false, rewrite it to make it true.

_____ 1. In 2000, Beckham won first place as World Footballer of the Year.

_____

_____ 2. Beckham joined the team of Manchester United as a teenager.

_____

_____ 3. Beckham is only famous as a soccer star.

_____

_____ 4. In 2003, Beckham became an Officer of the Order of the British Empire.

_____

_____ 5. Soccer is becoming more popular in the United States, especially among younger generations.

_____

_____ 6. Beckham was traded to the team Real Madrid in Spain for 41 million U.S. dollars.

_____

B. Number the sentences about David Beckham so they are in the correct time order.

_____ Beckham joined the team of Manchester United as a teenager.
_____ Beckham won the PFA Young Player of the Year award.
_____ David Beckham was born in 1975 in England.
_____ Beckham won second place as World Footballer of the Year.
_____ He became an Officer of the Order of the British Empire.
_____ Beckham married Victoria Adams.
_____ Beckham was traded to the team Real Madrid in Spain.

Test Your Vocabulary

C. Choose the word or phrase that best completes each sentence. Circle the letter.

1. Our school won the basketball _____ this year.
   a. nickname
   b. championship
   c. generation

2. Soccer wasn't as popular among people in my parents' _____.
   a. famous
   b. generation
   c. fashionable

3. My sister is a great _____. She plays soccer, tennis, and basketball.
   a. celebrity
   b. nickname
   c. athlete

4. We moved to Brazil when I was a _____. I went to high school in Rio.
   a. hit
   b. teenager
   c. athlete

5. France is _____ for its fine food and wine.
   a. famous
   b. fashionable
   c. celebrity

6. His first song was a big _____ as soon as it came out.
   a. championship
   b. nickname
   c. hit

7. B. B. King gave a(n) _____ performance at last night's concert.
   a. fashionable
   b. outstanding
   c. celebrity

8. Long skirts are _____ right now. Everyone is wearing them.
   a. hit
   b. famous
   c. fashionable

9. My sister's name is Margaret, but her _____ is Maggie.
   a. nickname
   b. hit
   c. celebrity

10. When someone becomes a _____, it's very difficult for him or her to have any privacy.
    a. famous
    b. championship
    c. celebrity

11. Who is the most _____ movie star in your country?

    a. famous

    b. nickname

    c. teenager

Using Context Clues

D. Read each of the sentences below. Try to guess the meaning of the underlined words. Do not use a dictionary.

1. In most of the world, Beckham is a major celebrity. He is a soccer <u>superstar</u> and one of the best English soccer players of all time.

    a. a famous person

    b. a player

    c. a reporter

2. In 1999, Beckham married a beautiful singer named Victoria Adams. Victoria was a <u>member</u> of the popular singing group the Spice Girls.

    a. a fan of

    b. a person in the group

    c. a bride

3. He dresses very well, and people like to <u>copy</u> his style. When Beckham gets a new style of haircut, it becomes a major news story. Soon lots of people are getting haircuts just like Beckham's.

    a. do the same thing as someone else

    b. laugh at something someone else does

    c. read about what someone has done

4. Now, there are surely children in the United States who <u>look up to</u> Beckham and dream of becoming the next David Beckham.

    a. dislike

    b. admire

    c. ignore

E. Choose four new words from the article "Beckham: A Soccer Superstar" that you want to learn and remember. Make a word map for each word.

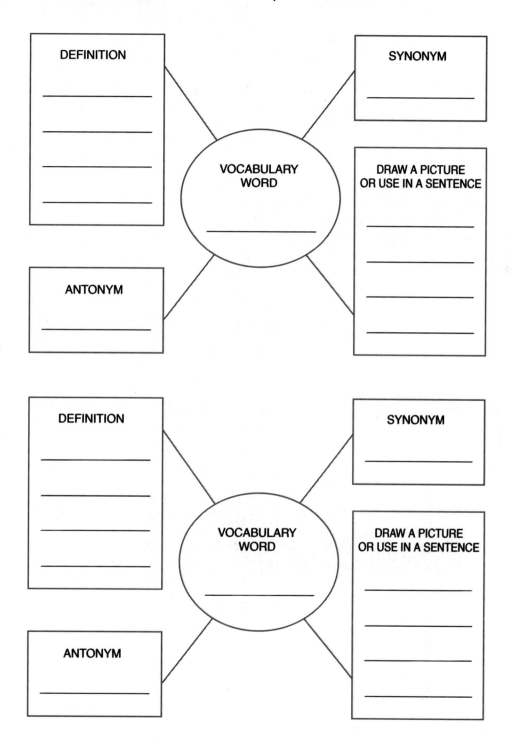

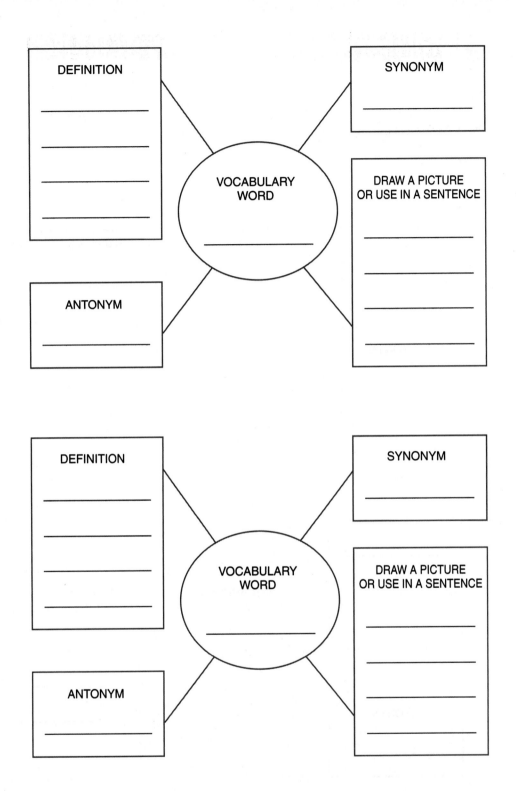

Share your word maps with a partner. Use them to teach your partner the meaning of the words.

Sharpen Your Vocabulary Skills

SUFFIXES

A **suffix** is a letter or group of letters added to the end of a word. Suffixes change the meaning of the word. Two common suffixes in English are *-er* and *-or*. They mean "someone who does something." For example, we can add the suffix *-er* to the word *sing* to make *singer,* someone who sings.

teach ⟶ teacher (someone who teaches)
sail ⟶ sailor (someone who sails)

A. Find three examples of words with the suffix *-er* in the article. Underline them.

B. Add the suffix *-er* or *-or* to make new words. Use your dictionary to check the spelling of the new words. Then write a sentence for each word.

> **Example**
>
> work <u>worker   He is a worker at the factory.</u>

1. invent _____

   _____

2. farm _____

   _____

3. build _____

   _____

4. visit _____

   _____

5. act _____

   _____

6. run _____

   _____

7. dictate _____

_____

8. create _____

_____

9. garden _____

_____

Another common suffix is *-ful*. The suffix *-ful* means "full of." It changes a noun into an adjective.

hope ⟶ hopeful (full of hope)

C. Find three examples of words with the suffix *-ful* in the article. Underline them.

D. Complete the sentences with a word with the suffix *-ful*.

> **Example**
>
> He takes a lot of care with his work. He is a <u>careful</u> worker.

1. My laptop computer has lots of uses. It is _____.

2. He always forgets to call me. He is a _____ person.

3. My sister helps everyone in the family. She is very _____.

4. My dentist has great skill at his work. He is a very _____ dentist.

5. The beauty of this painting is obvious. It is really _____ to look at.

6. The pyramids are one of the Seven Wonders of the World. They are _____.

7. The doctor said the operation was a success. The operation was _____.

8. She has many hopes about her future. She is _____ about her future.

9. The group sang with great joy. They sounded _____ when they sang.

WORK WITH WORDS

Phrasal Verbs

Many verbs in English are followed by a preposition, such as *of*, *up*, *on*, *to*, and so on. These two-part verbs are called **phrasal verbs**. The preposition that follows the verb changes the meaning of the verb. Sometimes a verb is followed by two prepositions. Look at the sentences from the article with phrasal verbs.

1. People all over the world have <u>heard of</u> him.
2. He <u>grew up</u> in London and joined the team of Manchester United as a teenager.
3. The new style <u>catches on</u>, and soon lots of people are getting haircuts just like Beckham's.
4. As they grow older, they <u>keep on</u> playing soccer.
5. Now, there are surely children in the United States who <u>look up to</u> Beckham and dream of becoming the next David Beckham.

A. Match the phrasal verbs in the left column with the correct definitions in the right column.

_____ **1.** hear of   **a.** to continue

_____ **2.** grow up   **b.** to admire and respect someone

_____ **3.** catch on   **c.** to know that something or someone exists because you have been told about it

_____ **4.** keep on   **d.** to develop from being a child to being an adult

_____ **5.** look up to   **e.** to become popular

B. Complete the sentences with the correct phrasal verb. Be sure to use the correct form of the verb.

1. I was born in Texas, but I _____ in Utah.
2. Jason _____ his older brother.
3. Do you think this new dance will _____ with younger people?
4. If he _____ studying, he will do well in the class.
5. Most teenagers have _____ the Beatles.

Pronoun Reference

C. Read the following sentences. Notice each underlined pronoun and look for the noun that it refers to.

1. David Beckham was born in 1975 in England. <u>He</u> joined the team of Manchester United as a teenager.

   He = _____

2. As a midfielder, Beckham helped both teams win many championships. <u>His</u> free kicks and skillful passing are outstanding.

   His = _____

3. Newspaper and television reporters love Beckham. <u>They</u> often talk and write about <u>his</u> clothes and haircuts.

   They = _____

   his = _____

4. When Beckham gets a new style of haircut, <u>it</u> becomes a major news story.

   it = _____

5. Victoria Adams was a member of the popular singing group the Spice Girls. <u>Her</u> name in this group was Posh Spice.

   Her = _____

6. Later that year, Queen Elizabeth gave England's highest honor to Beckham. <u>She</u> appointed <u>him</u> an Officer of the Order of the British Empire (OBE).

   She = _____

   him = _____

7. This same year, the movie *Bend It Like Beckham* became a popular hit. <u>It</u> was a wonderful movie about an English girl from an Indian family who dreams of becoming a successful soccer player.

   It = _____

8. More children are playing on soccer teams. As <u>they</u> grow older, <u>they</u> are watching more soccer matches and supporting the sport.

   they = _____

   they = _____

Word Families

D. Complete the following sentences with the correct word from the chart. Be sure to use the correct form of the word.

Noun	Verb	Adjective
popularity	popularize	popular
fashion	fashion	fashionable
cost	cost	costly
appointment	appoint	
success	succeed	successful
support	support	supportive

1. He always wears very _____ clothes.
2. How much does this car _____?
3. My uncle is a _____ doctor.
4. Which soccer team do you _____?
5. Beckham continues to gain _____.
6. He was _____ captain of the basketball team.
7. I hope you _____ in your new business.

Sum It Up

Reread "Beckham: A Soccer Superstar" and complete the summary.

David Beckham is one of the most famous _____ in the world. He has
                                              1
won many awards for his outstanding playing. He is also a _____.
                                                              2
Beckham is married to the singer _____. Beckham was born in _____,
                                     3   4
but he plays for a team in _____.
                              5

Express Your Ideas

A. Discuss these questions in small groups.

1. Do you play soccer now? If yes, what age were you when you began playing soccer? Is soccer popular with both males and females in your native country?

2. Who do you think is the most famous athlete in the world? What sport does he or she play?

3. How do you feel about the fact that professional athletes often become celebrities and make a great deal of money?

4. Why do you think soccer has traditionally been less popular in the United States than in the rest of the world?

B. Choose one of the questions above and write a paragraph about it.

_____

_____

_____

_____

_____

_____

Explore the Web

Do some research about your favorite athlete or an athlete you've read about. Use a search engine to explore the Web. Type in the name and check out some of the sites that look interesting to you. Make a list of five facts about the athlete you chose. Share the information with your classmates.

1. _____

2. _____

3. _____

4. _____

5. _____

Read Faster

Each row begins with a two-word expression. Circle the expressions in each row that are the same as the first expression. Don't worry if you see an expression you don't know. Just work as fast as you can. Try to complete the exercise in thirty seconds. When you have finished, check your answers on page 157. Figure out how many answers you got right and complete the chart on page 159. This will help you see your progress.

1.	tip top	top tip	tip tot	tip tie	tip top
2.	pick on	pick up	pick on	pick out	pick over
3.	keep out	keep on	keep out	keep up	keep to
4.	willy nilly	willy nitty	nilly witty	willy nilly	willy nifty
5.	wild ride	mild ride	wild rise	mild rise	wild ride
6.	pass out	pass on	past on	pass out	pass over
7.	catch on	catch on	catch it	cast off	cast it
8.	inside out	inside out	outside in	inside over	inside out
9.	let up	let us	lettuce	let down	let up
10.	helter skelter	halter skelter	helter skelter	skelter helter	hilter skelter

Have Some Fun

Work with a partner. One person is student A and uses the Student A chart on page 128. The other person is student B and uses the Student B chart on page 129. Do not look at your partner's chart. Fill in the missing pieces of information on your chart by asking your partner questions. For example, ask, "What sport does Hakeem play?" and "Where is Hakeem from?"

Name	Sport	Home Country
Hakeem Olajuwon	basketball	
José Santos		Chile
	wrestling	Russia
Tamura Ryoko		
	baseball	
Julio César Chávez	boxing	
	tennis	
		Korea
	soccer	
Bronko Nagurski		

Name	Sport	Home Country
		Nigeria
	jockey	
Alexander Karelin		
	judo	Japan
Pedro Martinez		Dominican Republic
		Mexico
Justine Henin-Hardenne		Belgium
Grace Park	golf	
Zinedine Zidane		France
	football	Canada

CHAPTER 7

Use the Clues
Making Inferences

Look at this photograph. Discuss it with a partner and then answer the questions that follow.

1. Based on what you see in the photo, which statements do you think are probably true? Check the boxes.

☐ The people are in a museum.

☐ They are meeting for the first time.

☐ The photo was taken many years ago.

☐ The women posed for the picture. (They knew they were being photographed.)

2. What do you think the relationship is between the man and the women? Why? _____

3. In what country do you think the sculpture was made? _____

4. In what year do you think this photo was taken? Why? _____

5. Why do you think this photo was taken? _____

When you looked at the photo, you gathered information about the people in the picture, the place, and the time period. You based the information on things you saw in the photo and your personal experience. In other words, you made inferences. You used what you knew and what you could see in the photo to make conclusions about things you could not see. In the same way, you can use information that is stated in a reading selection to make inferences about things that are not stated.

Sharpen Your Reading Skills

MAKING INFERENCES

We make inferences all the time in our everyday lives. For example, suppose you see your friend. He has a cast on his leg, and he is walking with crutches. What inference can you make about your friend? You can infer that he hurt his leg.

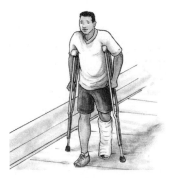

An inference is an educated guess you make based on information you know, see, or read. Look at the three pictures on the next page. The first person is watching TV. The second person is reading a book. The third person is watching a movie. Although we do not know the name of the TV show, book, or movie, we can make inferences about each one. We make the inferences based on the reaction of the person.

A. Look at the pictures below and answer the questions.

1. What kind of show do you think the boy is watching? _____

   Why? _____

2. What kind of book do you think the girl is reading? _____

   Why? _____

3. What kind of movie do you think the woman is watching? _____

   Why? _____

Good readers make inferences when they read. Writers don't always tell you everything they want you to know. Sometimes they just give you hints and clues. They expect you to figure out some things on your own. In other words, they want you to make inferences.

 An **inference** is an educated guess based on information in the reading. To make inferences you should combine the clues in the reading with information you already know from your own life.

B. Circle the letter of the inference you can make based on the information given.

> **Example**
>
> A boy goes into his house after walking home from school. He is carrying a wet umbrella.
>
> a. He washed his umbrella.
>
> (b.) It is raining outside.

1. A young woman nervously opens a letter. She reads it quickly, smiles, starts jumping up and down, and yells, "Yes!"
   a. She received good news.
   b. She got a letter from her mother.

2. You hear car horns honking. Soon you hear tires screeching, a loud crash, and the sound of breaking glass.
   a. There was a car accident nearby.
   b. Someone threw glass bottles out of his car window.

3. A couple and their two children get into a taxi. They have several suitcases. The man is carrying a camera. They tell the taxi driver to take them to the airport.
   a. The man is a professional photographer.
   b. The family is going on a trip.

4. Two students are in the library. They are looking at their class notes. They have their history textbooks open.
   a. They are studying.
   b. They are on a date.

5. A young woman walked into work and proudly showed her coworkers her new diamond ring. Everyone was smiling. Some people were hugging her.
   a. The woman loves her job.
   b. The woman just got engaged.

6. Martha sent invitations to all her friends. She cleaned her house and bought flowers. She made lots of food and bought things to drink. She picked out her favorite CDs and put up some decorations.

a. Martha is having a party.

b. Martha is moving to a new apartment.

C. Work with a partner. Take the role of A and B and read the following conversations aloud. Then answer the inference questions that follow.

1. **A:** Excuse me. I have to write a paper for my English class on the life of Agatha Christie. Can you help me find some information?

   B: I think you should start in the reference department with the computerized card catalog. Do you know how to use it?

   A: Yes, but where is the reference department?

   B: Just go up the stairs. It is the first room at the top of the stairs on your left. You'll see all the computers there and someone who can help you if you need it.

   1. Where do you think the conversation is taking place?

   2. What clues in the conversation helped you make your inference?

2. **A:** Hurry up! We don't want to miss the beginning.

   B: I am hurrying! Why don't you get in line here to buy tickets, and I'll go inside and buy some popcorn.

   A: OK. I'll meet you at the food stand.

   B: If you see Ellen and Jake, ask them to save us two seats. They said they were coming too.

   A: OK, please get me a soda, too.

   B: Fine. I'll see you in a few minutes.

   1. Where do you think the conversation is taking place?

   2. What clues in the conversation helped you make your inference?

3. **A:** How long has your tooth been hurting?

   B: Two weeks.

   A: Why didn't you come see me earlier?

   B: I thought it might get better. But, it's getting worse and worse.

A: Let me take a look. No wonder your tooth hurts. You have a big cavity. I'll fill it this week. Make an appointment with the receptionist.

B: Thanks.

1. Where do you think the conversation is taking place?
2. What clues in the conversation helped you make your inference?

4. **A:** Is everything OK here?

    B: This is cold.

    A: I'm sorry. I'll take it back to the kitchen for you and heat it up.

    B: It's also too salty. What other soups do you have today?

    A: Tomato, chicken with rice, and cream of mushroom.

    B: Let me try the tomato soup.

    A: I'll be right back with a new soup, sir.

1. Where do you think the conversation is taking place?
2. What clues in the conversation helped you make your inference?

5. **A:** Do you need some help?

    B: Yes, do you have these in size 7?

    A: I think so, but let me check. What color do you want?

    B: Black.

    A: Have a seat here and I'll be right back.

    B: Please bring them in brown too. I can't decide!

    A: Here you go. We have them in both colors.

    B: These feel too small. My feet hurt when I walk.

    A: Let me bring you size 7 $^1/_2$.

    B: Thanks.

1. Where do you think the conversation is taking place?
2. What clues in the conversation helped you make your inference?

D. Read the following paragraphs and choose the best inference for each one. Circle the correct letter.

1. Jack doesn't return Lillian's phone calls anymore. He also doesn't answer her e-mails. He walks on the other side of street when he sees her coming. Her friends have tried to talk to him, but he ignores them.

   a. Jack doesn't like to use e-mail.
   b. Lillian's friends are angry with Jack.
   c. Jack is angry with Lillian.

2. When Joanne got home from work she took two aspirin. She put on a sweater. Then she put on a coat. Then she turned the heat up in the apartment. When her sister Molly came home, she took Joanne's temperature and called the doctor.

   a. Joanne has a new sweater.
   b. Joanne is sick.
   c. Molly and the doctor are good friends.

3. After the game, all the players on the team and their parents were hugging and kissing each other. It was a great day in the history of the team. The coach took them all out for ice cream to celebrate.

   a. The team won the game.
   b. It was the first game of the season.
   c. Everyone on the team likes ice cream.

4. Jennifer is changing her spending habits. She is eating at home more often instead of going to restaurants. She is getting books from the library instead of buying them. She is wearing the clothes she has and not shopping for new clothes.

   a. Jennifer is trying to save money.
   b. Jennifer likes old clothes.
   c. Jennifer likes to cook.

Be an Active Reader

BEFORE YOU READ

A. What do you like to do when you go somewhere else? Check the things that are true for you. Then discuss your answers with a partner.

☐ Take pictures
☐ Meet new people
☐ Write in a journal
☐ Try new kinds of food
☐ Buy souvenirs

☐ Send postcards

☐ Go camping

☐ Stay in hotels

☐ Other: _____

B. **Discuss these questions with your partner.**

    1. Have you ever gone long distances by train? What are the advantages and disadvantages of going by train?

    2. Would you rather travel with a group of people on an organized tour or plan your own trip? Why?

    3. What do you think are the most interesting places in your home country?

Preview the Vocabulary

The words in the box are boldfaced in the journal entry. Work with a partner and do the exercise that follows.

Words to Watch

tour	guide	scenery
amazing	trail	wild
gorgeous	at least	scary
bottom	would rather	

C. **Read the following sentences. Then match the boldfaced words and phrases with the definitions on the next page. Write the correct letter in the space provided. If you need more help, read the sentence in the journal entry where the word appears and think about how it is used.**

_____ **1.** The sun is out, and there's a nice breeze. It's a **gorgeous** spring day.

_____ **2.** Our **guide** told us lots of interesting information about the history of Italy.

_____ **3.** I took pictures of the beautiful mountain **scenery**.

_____ **4.** The view at night from the balcony is **amazing**.

_____ **5.** As we walked along the **trail**, we picked some beautiful flowers.

_____ **6.** I'm afraid of **wild** animals. I'd rather see them at a zoo.

_____ **7.** We took a two-week **tour** of Italy.

_____ **8.** I need **at least** two hours to finish this work.

_____ **9.** The little boy cried in fright during the **scary** movie.

_____ **10.** Let's leave our car at the **bottom** of the mountain.

_____ **11.** I **would rather** go to New York by train than by bus.

a. making someone feel very surprised
b. the natural features of a place, such as mountains, forests, or lakes
c. not less than a particular number or amount
d. the lowest part of something
e. a path across open country or through a forest
f. very beautiful or pleasant
g. prefer
h. a trip in which you visit several different places in a country
i. living or growing in a natural state, and not controlled by people
j. someone who shows you the way to a place, especially to tourists
k. frightening

D. Match the name of the animal with the correct picture. Write the number in front of the name of the animal.

_____ buffalo   _____ moose   _____ bear   _____ elk   _____ mule

1.   2.   3.   4.   5.

E. Match the name with the correct picture. Write the number in front of the correct name.

_____ geyser   _____ mountains   _____ waterfall   _____ canyon

_____ cliff   _____ lake   _____ cave

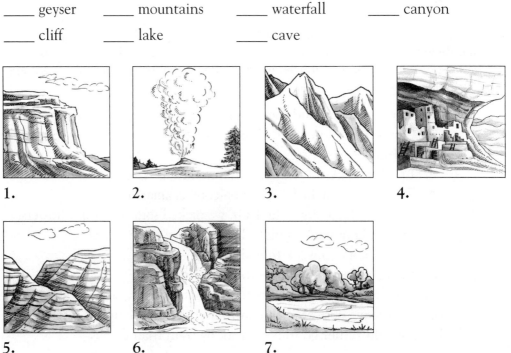

1.   2.   3.   4.

5.   6.   7.

Read with a Purpose

You are going to read the journal that a young woman wrote as she traveled by train to the National Parks of the western United States. Before you read the journal, complete the first two columns of the chart.

What I know about the western United States	What I want to know about the western United States	What I learned about the western United States

As you read the journal, think about inferences you can make. Put a check next to the statements in the boxes that are logical inferences.

My Travels by Train in the Western United States

1   *Chris and Jan wanted to visit the western United States. They decided to take a **tour** on a train called the American Orient Express. The tour included all their food and transportation. They even slept on the train, so they didn't have to make any hotel reservations. Chris and Jan wanted to learn about the history, native people, plants, and animals of the western United States. They were happy that there was a **guide** on the tour to explain everything to them.*

Thursday, June 12

2   We flew to Salt Lake City, Utah, this morning and got on the train at 3:00 P.M. The train is beautiful, but our room is very small (very, very small!). First we unpacked. Then we went to the observation car to meet the other people on our tour. Everyone goes there to meet people and enjoy the **scenery** through its huge windows. The people on our tour seem very nice, and I'm sure we'll make lots of new friends. Tomorrow when we wake up, we'll go to Yellowstone National Park in Wyoming.

```
_____ Chris and Jan are not from the western United States.
_____ Chris and Jan wanted to meet people.
_____ Chris and Jan are sisters.
```

Friday, June 13

3   We got to Yellowstone at 10:00 this morning. We saw huge
animals like buffalo, moose, bears, and elk, and smaller animals too.
They are all **wild** and free and fun to watch. Of course we had to see
Old Faithful, the most famous geyser in the world. Then a group of
us decided to hike[1] a few miles up to a beautiful waterfall. I found
some buffalo fur on the **trail**! It's silkier and softer than my cat's fur!
I'm going to save it. We saw and learned so much today and had lots
of fun with our new friends. Some people think Friday the 13th is an
unlucky day, but it was a great day for us! When we got back to the
train we were tired, but happy, and ready for a big dinner.

[1]**hike:** *to take a long walk in the country or mountains*

_____ Chris believes Friday the 13th is an unlucky day.
_____ Chris liked the buffalo fur.

Saturday, June 14

4   We woke up this morning at the Teton Mountains in western
Wyoming. What an **amazing** sight! The Tetons are part of the Rocky
Mountains. The highest point is called Grand Teton, and it is
unforgettable. We only went up to 11,000 feet, but the air up there
was thinner and colder than it was on the **bottom**. We hiked for
miles on a beautiful trail with lots of pretty flowers. The views of the
mountains and lakes and wild animals were unbelievable. I will
never forget how **gorgeous** the mountain scenery is here—especially
because I took so many pictures! I probably took too many, but I
couldn't stop until I ran out of film. By the time we got back on the
train, I was exhausted from walking so much. But I was ready for
another big dinner after another great day of great new experiences
with great new friends.

(Continued on next page.)

> _____ The Grand Teton is higher than 11,000 feet.
> _____ Chris took more pictures than Jan.

Sunday, June 15

5   We slept well as the train traveled to Utah and Zion National Park. No cars are allowed at Zion, so we walked or used the park bus to get around. Today was hotter than yesterday. It was 102 degrees Fahrenheit (38 degrees Centigrade). Our guide told us to bring **at least** a half-gallon of water to drink! We stayed at the bottom of the canyon and hiked along the river there. The view is amazing from the bottom. When I looked up at the rocks, I felt very small. They rise 3,000 feet (914 meters) toward the sky. Wind and water have changed the rocks into unusual shapes. Our guide said, "Nature is an amazing machine," and he was right. Jan pointed to two people climbing up the side of a rock. That looked **scary**. They were so high that it was hard to see them.

Monday, June 16

6   Today, Arizona: The Grand Canyon! Our guide pointed out that the Grand Canyon is not the widest, longest, or deepest canyon in the world, but it is the grandest. We hiked along an easy trail. I stayed on the trail, but Jan went off the trail to take pictures. She got very close to the edge. I told her it was unsafe, but I'm sure her pictures will be wonderful. Lots of people go by mule or on foot down to the bottom of the canyon. Not me, of course. Too scary! The Grand Canyon is a special place for Native Americans like the Hopi and the Navajo. They lived in the canyon a thousand years ago, and the land is still important to them. Today, they only go there for religious purposes. There is a lot to learn about the land and people of this area.

Tuesday, June 17

7   This morning we woke up in Albuquerque, New Mexico. After our usual big breakfast, we went to Bandelier National Monument. This is one of the places where the Anasazi Indians once lived. They made their homes in caves on the sides of high rock cliffs. How did they do that? It's not easy to get up to those caves. Our guide told us that the Anasazi first moved to this canyon in the late 1100s and stayed for about 400 years. The park has trails and ladders to make it easier for tourists to see inside some of the caves. I decided to be brave and climb up a 10-foot ladder to see inside a cave. I got to see the pictures the Anasazi drew on the walls so long ago. They were very interesting.

(Continued on next page.)

Naturally, Jan wanted to climb up to the highest cave—180 feet (55 meters) up! She's a lot braver than I am. Of course, I **would rather** stay on the ground and worry. Tonight was our farewell dinner. It was sad to say goodbye to these special friends after traveling so far with them. We all got along so well together. This was the most wonderful trip I've ever taken.

_____ Chris is afraid of heights.
_____ Jan is not afraid of heights.
_____ The Anasazi drew pictures of animals on the walls of the caves.

AFTER YOU READ

Fill in the third column in the chart on page 139. Did the journal answer any of your questions from the second column? Which ones? Look at the things you wrote in the first column. Were any of your ideas confirmed or rejected in the article? Which ones?

Check Your Comprehension

A. True or False? Write T (True) or F (False) next to each statement.

1. _____ Chris and Jan wanted to see the western United States.
2. _____ They had huge windows in their room.
3. _____ They saw only large animals at Yellowstone.
4. _____ The Grand Tetons are in Colorado like the Rocky Mountains.

5. _____ The rocks in Zion National Park were shaped by wind and water.
6. _____ The Grand Canyon is the deepest canyon in the world.
7. _____ Chris and Jan went by mule to the bottom of the Grand Canyon.
8. _____ The Anasazi Indians probably stayed in the Albuquerque, New Mexico area for 400 years.

B. Read each statement and decide if it is a fact or an opinion. Write F or O on the line.

_____ 1. It is easy to sleep on a train.
_____ 2. No cars are allowed in Zion National Park.
_____ 3. The Tetons are part of the Rocky Mountains.
_____ 4. The Grand Canyon is very beautiful.
_____ 5. The food served on the train is excellent.
_____ 6. The Anasazi Indians made their homes in caves on the sides of cliffs.
_____ 7. The best way to travel is to take a tour that includes food, transportation, and guides.
_____ 8. The Grand Tetons are unforgettable.

C. Scan the journal to find answers to the following questions.

1. At what time did Chris and Jan get on the train in Salt Lake City?
   _____

2. It was _____ degrees Centigrade in Zion National Park.

3. The rocks at Zion are approximately _____ feet (_____ meters) high.

4. How high was the ladder that Chris climbed? _____

5. What kinds of shapes did the Anasazi paint on the walls of their caves?
   _____

Test Your Vocabulary

D. Choose the word that best completes each sentence.

tour	guide	scenery
amazing	trail	scary
wild	gorgeous	bottom

1. My new computer is a(n) _____ machine.

2. This was a great _____ of England. Our _____ showed us where to go and explained all the interesting places to us.

3. I love to walk. Let's take a hike on this _____ next to the river.

4. I'm not brave enough to climb up this mountain. It's too _____ for me. I'll wait for you here at the _____.

5. At the zoo, I enjoy seeing the _____ animals up close.

6. Look out of the window. The _____ here is _____.

Using Context Clues

E. Read each of the sentences below. Try to guess the meaning of the underlined words. Do not use a dictionary.

1. No cars are <u>allowed</u> in the park. All visitors must walk or use the park bus to get around.

_____

2. By the time we got back on the train, I was <u>exhausted</u> from walking so much.

_____

3. I got to see the pictures the Anasazi <u>drew</u> on the walls so long ago.

_____

4. Tonight was our <u>farewell</u> dinner. It was sad to say goodbye to these special friends after traveling so far with them.

_____

F. Choose three new words from Chris's journal that you want to learn and remember. Make a word map for each word.

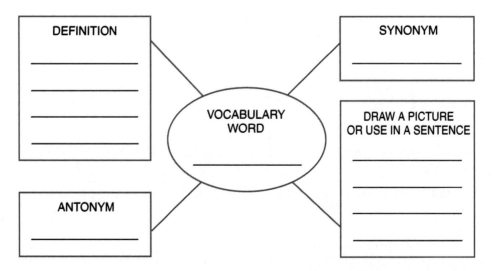

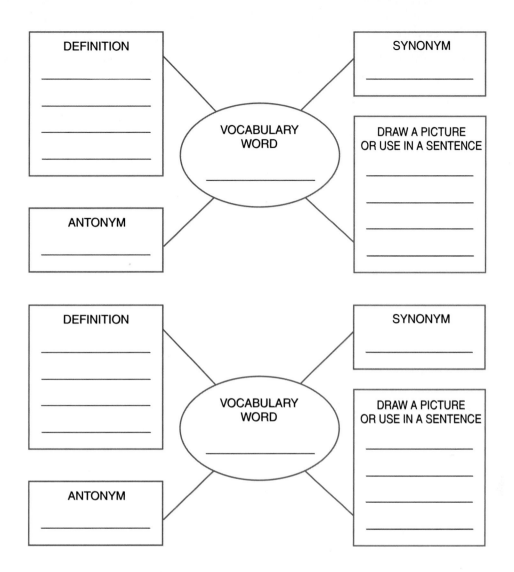

Share your word maps with a partner. Use them to teach your partner the meaning of the words.

Sharpen Your Vocabulary Skills

PREFIXES

A **prefix** is a group of letters that comes at the beginning of the word. A prefix changes the meaning of a word. Prefixes can help you learn the meanings of words. *Un–* is a common prefix in English. It means "not" or "the opposite of." Notice how the prefix *un–* changes the meaning of this sentence:

I am able to read this sentence. (I can read this sentence.)
I am unable to read this sentence. (I cannot read this sentence.)

A. Find five examples of words with the prefix *un-* in the article. Underline them.

B. Add the prefix *un-* to make new words. Use your dictionary to check the spelling of the new words. Then write a sentence for each word.

1. lock _____

   _____

2. necessary _____

   _____

3. comfortable _____

   _____

4. important _____

   _____

5. plug _____

   _____

WORK WITH WORDS

More Phrasal Verbs

Look at the sentences from the article with phrasal verbs.

1. We flew to Salt Lake City, Utah, this morning and <u>got on</u> the train at 3:00 P.M.

2. Tomorrow when we <u>wake up</u>, we'll go to Yellowstone National Park in Wyoming.

3. We <u>got to</u> Yellowstone at 10:00 this morning.

4. When we <u>got back</u> to the train we were tired, but happy, and ready for a big dinner.

5. I probably took too many, but I couldn't stop until I <u>ran out of</u> film.

6. All visitors must walk or use the park bus to <u>get around</u>.

7. We all <u>got along</u> so well together.

A. Match the phrasal verbs in the left column with the correct definitions in the right column.

_____ 1. get on   **a.** to stop sleeping

_____ 2. wake up   **b.** to arrive at a place

_____ **3.** get to   **c.** to move or travel to different places

_____ **4.** get back   **d.** to go onto a bus, train, airplane, or boat

_____ **5.** run out of   **e.** to have a friendly relationship with someone or a group of people

_____ **6.** get around   **f.** to return to a place

_____ **7.** get along   **g.** to use all of something, so that there is none left

B. Complete the sentences with the correct phrasal verb. Be sure to use the correct form of the verb.

1. I _____ early this morning.

2. She _____ very well with her mother-in-law.

3. I _____ sugar. Do you have some that I can borrow?

4. He is able to _____ well in his new wheelchair.

5. When I _____ the bus there were no seats left.

6. By the time I _____ to the hotel, Mary had already left.

7. When you _____ Spruce Street, turn left.

Irregular Verbs

C. Look at the list below of verbs with irregular past-tense forms from the article. Write the past tense of each verb. Then write a sentence for each word. You may need to use a dictionary to check the spelling.

1. sleep _____

_____

2. fly _____

_____

3. see _____

_____

4. wake _____

_____

5. make _____

_____

6. tell _____

_____

7. feel _____

_____

8. draw _____

_____

Synonyms and Antonyms

D. Write an S if the words are synonyms. Write an A if the words are antonyms. Use your dictionary to look up the meanings of unfamiliar words.

1. brave   cowardly   _____

2. gorgeous   beautiful   _____

3. bottom   top   _____

4. amazing   incredible   _____

5. trail   path   _____

Pronoun Reference

E. Read the following sentences. Notice each underlined pronoun and look for the noun that it refers to.

1. Some people think Friday the 13th is an unlucky day, but <u>it</u> was a great day for us!

it = _____

2. When you look up at the rocks, you feel overwhelmed. <u>They</u> rise 3,000 feet (914 meters) toward the sky.

They = _____

3. Our guide said, "Nature is an amazing machine," and <u>he</u> was right.

he = _____

4. Jan pointed to two people climbing up the side of a rock. That looks scary! <u>They</u> were so high that it was hard to see <u>them</u>.

They = _____

them = _____

5. After our usual big breakfast, we went to Bandelier National Monument. <u>This</u> is one of the places where the Anasazi Indians once lived. <u>They</u> made their homes in caves on the sides of high rock cliffs.

This = _____

They = _____

6. I got to see the pictures the Anasazi drew on the walls so long ago. <u>They</u> were very interesting.

They = _____

Sum It Up

A. A summary gives only main ideas. It does not include too many details. Before you write your summary, think about who, when, where, why, what, and how. Answer these questions.

1. Who traveled? _____

2. Where did they go? _____

3. How did they get there? _____

4. Why did they take the trip? _____

5. What did they see? _____

_____

B. Use the answers to the questions to write a summary of Chris's journal.

_____

_____

_____

_____

_____

_____

_____

Express Your Ideas

A. Discuss these questions in small groups.

1. Do you like to go new places and see new things or do you prefer to stay home and relax when you have vacation time?

2. Do you like to write? Do you write about new experiences in a journal? Do you like to take photos?

3. Have you visited any national parks in your home country? In the United States If yes, which ones? What did you like or dislike about them?

4. Have you studied early people in your country? Share information about the history of the early people in your country with your classmates.

5. What is your impression of Chris and Jan? How would you describe them? Do you think they are adventurous? Interesting? What other adjectives would you use to describe them?

B. Choose one of the questions above and write a paragraph about it.

_____

_____

_____

_____

_____

_____

_____

_____

_____

_____

Explore the Web

Use the Internet to find out the height and location of each of these mountains in both feet and meters.

Mountain	Country	Height in Feet	Height in Meters
1. Aconcagua			
2. Mount Fuji			
3. Mount Cook			
4. Mount Kilimanjaro			
5. Grand Teton			
6. Mont Blanc			
7. Vinson Massif			
8. Mount Everest			
9. Mount Vesuvius			
10. Mount Olympus			

Read Faster

Each row begins with a two-word expression. Circle the expressions in each row that are the same as the first expression. Don't worry if you see an expression you don't know. Just work as fast as you can. Try to complete the exercise in thirty seconds. When you have finished, check your answers on page 158. Figure out how many answers you got right and complete the chart on page 159. This will help you see your progress.

1. pen pal	pen pat	pal pen	pen pal	pen pals
2. high school	higher school	height school	school work	high school
3. bird's eye	early birds	bird's eye	easy bird	bird's eyes
4. take off	take out	takes out	take off	taken off

5.	two cents	too cents	to cents	two cent	two cents
6.	cut out	cut off	put out	cut out	cut in
7.	close call	close calls	class call	call close	close call
8.	first name	first fame	fist name	last name	first name
9.	good book	good book	good hook	good books	great book
10.	long face	long lace	long song	long face	lonely face

Have Some Fun

Can you find your way through the maze to the Eiffel Tower?

Read Faster

CHAPTER 1

1. might	fight	bright	light	(might)	tight	right
2. corn	horn	corner	torn	(corn)	born	core
3. fit	fine	five	lit	(fit)	fix	fist
4. stair	stain	steal	store	stale	stick	(stair)
5. burn	bush	turn	(burn)	busy	stern	learn
6. ring	thing	rings	think	sing	king	(ring)
7. owe	owl	out	over	owes	(owe)	own
8. hand	has	hat	hand	(head)	heat	heavy
9. pack	peak	(pack)	packed	pace	peace	pad
10. exit	exist	exits	expect	excel	(exit)	except

CHAPTER 2

1. near	nearly	next	nest	never	nearer	(near)
2. law	lax	lawn	(law)	raw	late	rate
3. pick	tick	trick	pack	picky	pickle	(pick)
4. dish	(dish)	disk	dirt	fish	fast	dishes
5. fear	feet	ear	tear	gear	(fear)	feel
6. pie	lie	(pie)	peace	pit	pick	tie
7. tall	talk	tail	ten	tell	tan	(tall)
8. eye	end	oil	eight	eyes	(eye)	eight
9. mix	milk	mock	model	fix	(mix)	mixed
10. have	had	heaven	heavy	(have)	hats	head

CHAPTER 3

1. pint   pine   pinch   pin   (pint)   pile   pike

2. deep   deem   deal   deed   deepen   (deep)   deeply

3. cameo   camera   calm   camp   came   campus   (cameo)

4. does   (does)   don't   dean   deep   doll   donut

5. teeth   tooth   tool   team   (teeth)   teal   time

6. said   sake   sail   say   sad   (said)   sale

7. book   boor   boot   boat   boom   books   (book)

8. license   silence   liver   (license)   sliver   slice   lichen

9. dessert   desert   despot   destroy   (dessert)   destiny   distinct

10. laugh   laud   launch   launder   laughter   laundry   (laugh)

CHAPTER 4

1. well-made   well-said   (well-made)   poorly made   (well-made)

2. look up   (look up)   look over   look at   (look up)

3. work out   walk out   (work out)   (work out)   work on

4. make up   (make up)   made up   make out   (make up)

5. get in   (get in)   get it   got in   (get in)

6. rain hat   brain hat   (rain hat)   rain hard   (rain hat)

7. summer school   (summer school)   summer vacation   (summer school)   ski school

8. candy bar   (candy bar)   candy cane   candy bag   (candy bar)

9. flat tire   flat time   (flat tire)   free tire   (flat tire)

10. tall tale   telltale   (tall tale)   (tall tale)   tall tile

CHAPTER 5

1. put on	put out	put over	(put on)	put in
2. tree top	tee top	top tee	top tree	(tree top)
3. take out	(take out)	take on	take over	take it
4. sweet treat	sweat treat	(sweet treat)	sweet tree	sweat tree
5. get up	get on	get over	(get up)	get it
6. get along	get alone	get it	(get along)	get up
7. flower power	flowing power	power flower	flower tower	(flower power)
8. fill out	fill in	(fill out)	felt it	fill it
9. tip off	tip top	tip toe	(tip off)	tip over
10. topsy turvy	topsy turkey	turvy topsy	topsy turny	(topsy turvy)

CHAPTER 6

1. tip top	top tip	tip tot	tip tie	(tip top)
2. pick on	pick up	(pick on)	pick out	pick over
3. keep out	keep on	(keep out)	keep up	keep to
4. willy nilly	willy nitty	nilly witty	(willy nilly)	willy nifty
5. wild ride	mild ride	wild rise	mild rise	(wild ride)
6. pass out	pass on	past on	(pass out)	pass over
7. catch on	(catch on)	catch it	cast off	cast it
8. inside out	(inside out)	outside in	inside over	inside out
9. let up	let us	lettuce	let down	(let up)
10. helter skelter	halter skelter	(helter skelter)	skelter helter	hilter skelter

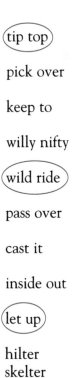

1. pen pal   pen pat   pal pen   (pen pal)   pen pals

2. high school   higher school   height school   school work   (high school)

3. bird's eye   early birds   (bird's eye)   easy bird   bird's eyes

4. take off   take out   takes out   (take off)   taken off

5. two cents   too cents   to cents   two cent   (two cents)

6. cut out   cut off   put out   (cut out)   cut in

7. close call   close calls   class call   call close   (close call)

8. first name   first fame   fist name   last name   (first name)

9. good book   (good book)   good hook   good books   great book

10. long face   long lace   long song   (long face)   lonely face

Read Faster

	CORRECT ANSWERS									
	1	2	3	4	5	6	7	8	9	10
CHAPTER 1										
CHAPTER 2										
CHAPTER 3										
CHAPTER 4										
CHAPTER 5										
CHAPTER 6										
CHAPTER 7										